Polymorphous Domesticities

FLASHPOINTS

The series solicits books that consider literature beyond strictly national and disciplinary frameworks, distinguished both by their historical grounding and their theoretical and conceptual strength. We seek studies that engage theory without losing touch with history and work historically without falling into uncritical positivism. FlashPoints aims for a broad audience within the humanities and the social sciences concerned with moments of cultural emergence and transformation. In a Benjaminian mode, FlashPoints is interested in how literature contributes to forming new constellations of culture and history and in how such formations function critically and politically in the present. Available online at http://repositories.cdlib.org/ucpress.

Series Editors

Ali Behdad (Comparative Literature and English, UCLA)

Judith Butler (Rhetoric and Comparative Literature, UC Berkeley), Founding Editor

Edward Dimendberg (Film & Media Studies, UC Irvine), Coordinator

Catherine Gallagher (English, UC Berkeley), Founding Editor

Jody Greene (Literature, UC Santa Cruz)

Susan Gillman (Literature, UC Santa Cruz)

Richard Terdiman (Literature, UC Santa Cruz)

1. *On Pain of Speech: Fantasies of the First Order and the Literary Rant,* by Dina Al-Kassim
2. *Moses and Multiculturalism,* by Barbara Johnson, with a foreword by Barbara Rietveld
3. *The Cosmic Time of Empire: Modern Britain and World Literature,* by Adam Barrows
4. *Poetry in Pieces: César Vallejo and Lyric Modernity,* by Michelle Clayton
5. *Disarming Words: Empire and the Seductions of Translation in Egypt,* by Shaden M. Tageldin
6. *Wings for Our Courage: Gender, Erudition, and Republican Thought,* by Stephanie H. Jed
7. *The Cultural Return,* by Susan Hegeman
8. *Reading Delhi: The Politics of Language and Literary Production in India,* by Rashmi Sadana
9. *The Cylinder: Kinematics of the Nineteenth Century,* by Helmut Müller-Sievers
10. *Polymorphous Domesticities: Pets, Bodies, and Desire in Four Modern Writers,* by Juliana Schiesari

Polymorphous Domesticities

Pets, Bodies, and Desire in Four Modern Writers

Juliana Schiesari

UNIVERSITY OF CALIFORNIA PRESS
Berkeley · Los Angeles · London

University of California Press, one of the most
distinguished university presses in the United States,
enriches lives around the world by advancing
scholarship in the humanities, social sciences, and
natural sciences. Its activities are supported by the UC
Press Foundation and by philanthropic contributions
from individuals and institutions. For more
information, visit www.ucpress.edu.

University of California Press
Berkeley and Los Angeles, California

University of California Press, Ltd.
London, England

© 2012 by The Regents of the University of California

Library of Congress Cataloging-in-Publication Data

Schiesari, Juliana.
   Polymorphous domesticities : pets, bodies, and
desire in four modern writers / Juliana Schiesari.
      p. cm. – (Flashpoints ; 10)
   Includes bibliographical references and index.
   ISBN 978-0-520-27084-8 (pbk. : alk. paper)
   1. Animals in literature.   2. Wharton, Edith,
1862-1937–Criticism and interpretation.   3. Barnes,
Djuna–Criticism and interpretation.   4. Colette,
1873-1954–Criticism and interpretation.   5. Ackerley,
J. R. (Joe Randolph), 1896-1967–Criticism and
interpretation.   6. Pets in literature.
7. Human-animal relationships in literature.
8. Sex (Psychology) in literature.   9. Social
structure in literature.   10. Social values in
literature.   I. Title.   II. Title: Pets, bodies, and desire
in four modern writers.
   PN56.A64.S25 2011
   809'.93362–dc23
                                        2011027809

21 20 19 18 17 16 15 14 13 12
10   9   8   7   6   5   4   3   2   1

*For Angelica
and all the wonderful animals*

Contents

Acknowledgments ix

Introduction 1
1. Re-Visions of Diana in Edith Wharton 16
2. Colette at Home 38
3. Romancing the Beast: J.R. Ackerley's Dog Days
   and the Meaning of Sex 76
   Afterword 114

Notes 117
Bibliography 127

Acknowledgments

This book reflects my long-standing interest on the subject of nonhuman animals as a literary project but also, and foremost, as domestic friends and companions.

I am deeply indebted to many colleagues and friends for their support of my work as well as for their generosity in pointing me toward some of the authors whose literary works are the subject of this book. I owe a special thanks to Laura Mulvey, who first told me about the incredible opus and world of J. R. Ackerley, and to Kari Lokke, who brought my attention to the extraordinary work of Colette and her menagerie. I also owe Georges Van Den Abbeele thanks for his careful attention to detail, astute readings, and editorial skills.

Heartfelt gratitude goes to Brenda Schildgen, Bob Schildgen, and Julia Simon, who read parts of the manuscript as I was preparing to send it off to UC Press. Their invaluable comments, suggestions, and editorial acumen undoubtedly helped turn the manuscript into its present form. It is also a pleasure to thank all those who, in many ways, contributed to its publication: Barbara Spackman, Carla Freccero, Christina Schiesari, Nancy Schiesari, Clarence Walker, Tim Murray, Renate Ferro, Gail Finney, Natalie Strobach, Mike Graziano, and all my colleagues in comparative literature and in French and Italian for their support over the years for this project. I have been fortunate to enjoy and share many conversations with Carla Freccero, Barbara Spackman, Brenda

Schildgen, and Julia Simon on the subject of sharing life and domestic spaces with our animal companions.

I owe a tremendous debt of gratitude to Barbara Spackman and an anonymous reader at the Press whose comments and suggestions helped turn this manuscript into a much stronger and more coherent book. I am ever grateful to Dick Terdiman for believing in this work and for gently shepherding it as it went through its various stages toward publication. I also thank Elisabeth Magnus for her careful editorial work. Finally, I wish to thank the Flashpoints committee and the University of California Press board for their support in the publication of this book.

No words can adequately express the life-sustaining energy that my daughter Christina, my granddaughter Angelica, and our animal companions have meant to me. While enduring one of the worst crises in our lives. they managed to keep me focused on the manuscript and brought much and continued joy despite our common suffering. I am ever thankful and most fortunate to have them in my life.

Introduction

It is interesting that in the country in almost every village there is a man who has not married. . . . Nobody can take him very seriously, they often call him familiarly, a hen, and most of the time he does go a little funny. . . .

There are of course some women not often more than one in a village who has not married, but she is not so likely in France to go funny, of course there are always animals, and animals can become a family, to a Frenchwoman, but not to a Frenchman.

—Gertrude Stein, *Paris, France*

This book continues the exploration I began in *Beasts and Beauties: Animals, Gender and Domestication in the Italian Renaissance* concerning the co-development of two different but related forms of domestication since the Renaissance: the new culture of domesticated animals that issued forth in the modern phenomenon of the "pet," and the contemporaneous delineation of the home as a uniquely private enclosure, where the *pater familias* ruled over his own secluded world of domesticated wife, children, servants—and animals.[1] The early modern invention of the pet, I argue, takes place squarely within the simultaneous negotiation of modern family relations that have long defined the unequal status of men, women, and the beings who live with them.[2] The relations between domesticity and power that have emerged in Euro-American societies since the Renaissance have drawn on a wide set of ideological affinities between "femininity," "sexuality," and "animality" in ways that continue to frame our understanding of how different personal, social, sexual, and species identities are formed and valued today. The patriarchal norm of the modern family with homebound women, children, and pets is, like any norm, only a social convention, an imagined ideological ideal that may often be undermined in practice. Yet departing from the norm, even ever so slightly, can bring real risks. As Stein's quip underscores, men without a domesticated realm to rule lose—at least "in France"—not just their masculinity but their very humanity: they become "hens" and "go a little funny." Women, specifically French women, however, can create their own, alternative domestic space of animals (and, why not, of other women, children, perhaps even some men).[3] Stein remains upbeat about this possibility here, but history tells otherwise. The spinster on the edge of town with a few too many cats or dogs has all too often served as the stereotype of the witch with her devilish familiars, who then becomes all too easily persecuted for living outside normative gender codes.[4] There are, in short, ways to resist the patriarchal paradigm with the establishment of alternative domesticities, but with varying risks as well as positive possibilities. To the extent that norms are themselves representational constructs (socially accredited and prescribed idealizations), literature, in particular, provides an especially propitious domain for the imaginary exploration of different representations. Recently, Carla Freccero has insightfully argued for an understanding of literature as the representation of a "figural, fantasmatic, historiographic practice that attends to the way that topoi—discursive commonplaces—haunt texts across historical eras to address the non-causal, non-linear relation of events and *affects*. . . . Their relay between times and places looks more like a haunting—an affective insistence, persistence, a spectral materialization—than a progression, a borrowing, or a coming after" (emphasis mine).[5]

This book maps out such a "figural" play of gender, sexuality, and alternative forms of domesticity in four modern European and American writers: Edith Wharton, Djuna Barnes, Colette, and J.R. Ackerley. Why these four? They are certainly not representative of some movement or trend, intellectual or artistic. What they do have in common is a defiance of the patriarchal paradigm in the lives they led as well as the literature that represents those lives, as "an affective insistence" on difference.[6] Not only did the four above-mentioned writers live outside the norms of the heterosexual family unit, but the alternative lifestyles they led and wrote about also in every case prominently involved animals of various kinds and in as many capacities.[7] Their rearrangements of the family order unsurprisingly explored sexual alternatives (homoeroticism, bestiality) as well as domestic ones. They were, of course, not the only mavericks in a modernity marked by cultural, sexual, and social experimentation, but their pursuit of alternatives in direct concert with animals motivates my critical attention in this book.

Indeed, a primary aim of this study is to consider how anxieties about gender and sexuality have been expressed through the language and figures of animals and animality within literature and/or through the direct involvement of animals with humans and how that involvement has been interpreted by humans. In other words, does a human who "loves" his or her "pet" remain anthropocentric or cross a line into a "beastly" relation that disturbs the binary distinction between human and nonhuman?

. . .

While the works I study by Wharton and Colette overtly enact the deconstruction of the traditional familial order through the intrusion of the animal inside domestic space, those by Barnes and Ackerley also explore the erotic consequences of desire and intimacy, exploding in the process conventional notions about what is or is not sexuality. While homoeroticism figures prominently in these writings, it appears less as a ground of sexual or social identity per se (suggestive, for example, of some inherent link between being gay and liking animals) than as a transitional space that opens up the wide field of polymorphous possibilities beyond heterosexist normativity. Ackerley's case is most noteworthy in this regard for his abandonment of a committed gay lifestyle to pursue a different kind of "relationship" with a female German shepherd dog, to the consternation of everyone from his own sister to prominent gay friends like E.M. Forster. Likewise, Colette's lesbian explorations point beyond her oppressive marriage with Willy to the exploding of domestic space in works like *La maison de Claudine,* which model home environments where women, men, children, pets, livestock, and even "wild" animals interact in all manner of dehierarchized and unscripted ways. The utopian alternative is thus a kind of polymorphous domesticity, a concept I model on the psychoanalytic concept of polymorphous perversity as the preexisting ground of all eroticism prior to the repressions that prescribe heteronormative sexuality.[8] In the same way, a polymorphous domesticity is represented in spaces of familial intimacies and interspecies communality unrestricted by the Renaissance paradigm of the patriarchal home.

My point in analyzing the overlap between figures of women (and men) and figures of animals is not just to reexamine certain stereotypical correlations in modern culture—for example, between a decadent femininity and animality—but to reassess the relations between culture and domination as evidenced through paradigms of representation that apply to all those entities, whether human beings of other genders, ethnicities, and sexualities or "nonhuman" creatures, that are viewed as needing to be "domesticated." While this book remains focused on a European/North American context, which allows me the opportunity to track the later historical revisions of the paradigm studied in my exploration of "beasts and beauties" in the Italian Renaissance, I fully imagine further work that would explore these same questions in the very different contexts of other cultures, especially with attention to issues of race and ethnicity in colonial as well as postcolonial situations.

I hope not to "exploit" the representation of animals by reducing their meaning to mere ciphers of human interaction like the stereotypical attributes of human behavior represented by the animal characters that appear in fables, a stereotyping that raises the question of anthropocentrism by scientists and others interested in animal behavior. On the other hand, the scientific study of animals in their "isolation" may not be any less anthropocentric in its refusal to see any relations between humans and animals. Rather, it is precisely the *relation* between human and animal that interests me. As anthropologists have long argued, the nature/culture divide takes place *within* culture. One could even say, following this kind of logic, that there exists no animal "outside" culture. After all, it is our language and our systems of thought that represent the animal. Though some behaviorists or biologists have claimed that scientific methodology allows for the "pure understanding" of animal behavior, I would argue, instead, that it is the analysis of the *relation* between humans and animals that needs understanding. And this relation is far more meaningful than the simple deconstruction of such binarisms as "good" or "bad" (literary or scientific, mythical or analytic, well intentioned or cynical, ecological or exploitative, etc.) that the representations of animals per se would suggest. Rather, it involves the modalities and ethics of human-animal interaction, the "economy" of the animal within human cultures, and especially the role of nonrational processes in the rapprochement of certain specific humans with certain specific animals.

Perhaps it is precisely from the category of an "excluded other" that a rethinking of the representation of animals can produce a different but (hopefully) valuable consideration of the role animals play in our human lives, especially at the level of our domestic involvement with them. By *domestic*, I mean the animals that we humans bring into our lives, as companions and friends but also as objects of research and objects of our gaze. I hope to show that a discourse about animals and how they intersect with our lives need not be one of appropriating their integrity but can be one that allows for differences of species to emerge at the same time that a relation does indeed exist, one based on a mutual projection of care and emotional investment into one's other. This relation provides the most salient alternative to any anthropocentric mode of expression. It is what the French philosophers and psychoanalysts Gilles Deleuze and Félix Guattari imply by their notion of "*devenir-animal*."[9] The ground of "humanist" thought then appears in retrospect inherently "speciest," that is, asserting the primacy and superiority of humans over all other creatures, but this fundamental "speciesism" in turn guides and serves as the model for the development of various *intra*-species claims to hierarchy, including racism, sexism, classism, and other forms of institutionalized ideologies of privilege and "normativity." Small wonder that today's postmodernist critical theory, after dismantling humanist mythology through the deconstruction of racism, sexism, et al., has apparently found the ultimate ground of its antihumanism in the species boundary between the human and what Lyotard calls the "inhuman," or, as mentioned above, in what Deleuze and Guattari call "*devenir-animal*."[10]

Such "posthumanist" investigations are now making powerful connections with the expanding field of what has come to be called "animal studies." To understand better what that field means, one could propose the following rough typology of its major thematic concerns. The oldest and strongest line of inquiry is no doubt the one engaged in the long-standing debate over whether and in what capacity animals can be said to have "rights."[11] It has moved from a stance, increasingly viewed as anthropomorphic, that simply extends the human and legal concept of rights to nonhuman beings to more nuanced discussions about animal "welfare" and human responsibility. A second and somewhat related major line of inquiry concerns the cognitive and emotional life of animals; it is spearheaded by the likes of Vicki Hearne and Jeffrey Masson and is currently well represented by scholars like Marc Bekoff and Marian Stamp Dawkins.[12] I will return to this issue in a moment, since the critical relation between animal "feelings" and anthropomorphism directly affects a study such as this one, based in analysis of literary texts. Finally, in the area of studying the representation and social construction of animals in human art and culture, considerable work has also been done, though chiefly with a historical approach.[13] Feminist interventions have not been lacking either.[14]

All these strands are brought most powerfully together in two crucial thinkers, who must be viewed as a class all their own: Cary Wolfe and Donna Haraway. Haraway, in a series of influential meditations from *Primate Visions* to *The Companion Species Manifesto* to *When Species Meet,* comes at the question of the animal from a critical science studies perspective that radically decenters humanist anthropocentrism. Wolfe, on the other hand, represents the most sophisticated distillation of the poststructuralist contribution to the question in a stunning variety of publications that take the insights of Derrida, Deleuze, and others to a new level of coherence and critical energy.[15]

Humanist privilege and posthumanist imagination are directly relevant to this current study, especially as questions of animal cognition and sensitivity interact with various forms of anthropomorphic projection in the represented context that is the literary text. We can begin by returning to some of the fundamental tenets of humanist thought and its concomitant assertion of human privilege, and indeed dominance, over all other forms of life. Atop the list of the disdained others of humanism's claim to rationality and scientific reason as superior modes of thinking are, of course, sentiment and feeling. Curiously, while scientific discussion of animal consciousness is reluctant to posit anything beyond instinctual intelligence, the question of so-called animal emotions is a lively area of debate, all the more so for the emotional pull animals are observed to exert over human beings (even those human beings closed to most other emotional influences). There appears little discussion of whether any animals "think" but plenty of discussion over whether and what animals "feel." Perhaps the acrimony of debate over the meaning behind the weeping of elephants or the howling of wolves involves the incremental relation to rationality implied by emotion itself. For emotional display as understood by classic Western humanism is not so much the opposite of reason as its inept use by lesser humans, namely women and members of subordinated classes, ethnicities, or races, for these are stereotypically those who are seen to laugh or cry too easily; to be excessively manipulated by sympathy or antipathy; to gesticulate too much and talk too loudly; to eat, drink, and sleep too much; and so on. In other words, the degree of one's rational self-mastery signifies one's place within a social hierarchy of power and privilege. On the one hand, emotionality designates one as less human, thereby closer to the animal world; on the other hand, animals' "emotions" situate them closer to human beings than humanism would care for, suggesting a precarious continuum between human and nonhuman creatures rather than a clearly delineated and comfortably insuperable divide between them. Emotion, as a kind of liminal rationality, thus offers a kind of oxymoronic fulcrum from which to rethink categories inherited from Renaissance thought, such as the mind/body split, most overtly associated with the name of René Descartes.[16]

And while Descartes might represent the most strident anthropocentric humanism, in which animals, far from being alternate forms of life (whether "rational" or not), are mere machines under the blind direction of the laws of physics and nature, it would be incorrect to attribute this view to all humanist thinkers. In the same way that early humanism, as I have often argued, co-presents sexism and misogyny, racism and egalitarianism, we find proponents of the animal world such as Leonardo da Vinci, whose principled vegetarianism and love of animals suggest his more modest appraisal of humanity's place in the natural order, or Michel de Montaigne, whose skeptical treatise the "Apology for Raymond Sebond" abounds in examples of animal behavior and consciousness that equal or exceed their human correlatives, culminating in his famous question: "When I play with my cat, who knows if I am not a pastime to her more than she is to me?"[17]

Exponents of such (un)humanist positions often find themselves tarred by their more doctrinally humanistic brethren with the accusation of "anthropomorphism," or the unjustifiable projection of uniquely human qualities onto animals. The uses and abuses of anthropomorphism are still a primary focus of debate among those who study animal behavior today. In *Animal Rights and the Politics of Literary Representation,* John Simons makes a useful distinction between "trivial" and "strong" anthropomorphism. For Simons, trivial anthropomorphism would include the treatment of animals as if they were people, such as we typically find in writings for children or fables.[18] We can also see trivial anthropomorphism in everyday life, where, for example, people dress their "pets" to mirror human rituals (such as marriage rites) or train them to perform human tasks such as using a toilet. This sort of anthropomorphism is less a projection than an appropriation and a forcible "morphing" of animals into a human image, a literal anthropo-*morphism*. Such a denial of creatural "identity" (however loosely speaking) is not merely absurd but unethical and wrong—just as the appropriation of one culture by another denies the differences as well as similarities between them and erases the borrowed other's integrity while abjecting it from its own discourse. On the other hand, the *absolute* rejection of anthropomorphism constructs an intellectual and emotional "firewall" between humans and other creatures, implicitly reducing them to the level of things or property to be bought, sold, or used at will (a point of view culminating in modern industrialized farming, which is as dehumanizing to the people involved in it as it is unspeakably brutal to the animals, whose very existence is reduced to their "production value").

The essays in an interesting volume titled *Anthropomorphism, Anecdotes, and Animals* take various positions on the question of anthropomorphism: some view it as enabling and some do not. Some criticize anthropomorphism as inherently anthropocentric, but none adequately deconstruct the very premise of their articulations.[19] Uncritically accepting a binary opposition between advocating and rejecting anthropomorphism, they seem determined not to see that the opponents of anthropomorphism, by surreptitiously granting the human subject the privileged position of surveyor of the uncontaminated "truth" of behavior, make the human subject central to itself and to its project—a position every bit *as anthropocentric* as the worst excesses of anthropomorphism.

The fear of anthropomorphism, I believe, is again the fear of being connected to anything outside the human, the fear that any common ground of similarity (just like any smidgen of so-called "reason") would bring down the entire edifice of human culture. Likewise, the rejection of anthropomorphism in scientific discourse typically masks an anthropomorphism that lurks at the very core of animal research, namely that discoveries made in the course of experiments on animals will cross over into benefits for humans. The justification for using white mice, for example, other than their size, ease of handling, and rapid reproductive cycles (the real reasons they are so prized in labs!) is that their DNA is said to be closer than most other creatures' to that of humans. This similarity of molecular *form* (i.e., an anthropo-*morphism* between mice and humans) is supposed to mean a higher level of crossover, yet more often than not, discoveries made in animal research do not readily apply to human cases, as evidenced by repeated blind alleys in medical research for alleged human benefit.

Finally, bearing in mind Nietzsche's infamous remark about truth being a "mobile army of metaphors, metonymies and anthropomorphisms," one must ask whether human language can escape anthropomorphism.[20] To speak outside anthropomorphism may be as impossible as the claim to step outside culture to reach a pure state of nature. Moreover, are not the intersubjective processes of projection and introjection part of the human process of affection, attachment, and cognition?[21] The very positing of these processes prompts the question of whether animals also project and introject. Probably, but the degree to which we *cannot* know and can instead only speculate through anecdotes and literature, through a "feeling" subject, suggests the need to acknowledge human limitations in understanding other creatures, as Leonardo da Vinci and Montaigne tried so long ago to tell us.

There is another way, however, to conceive of the issue, suggested by what Simons terms a "strong" anthropomorphism, or what I would prefer to call a "self-reflective" anthropomorphism. Self-reflective anthropomorphism is justified because it points not only to the similarities between humans and animals but also to their differences, displaying an intersubjectivity that does not deny the radical uniqueness of each species. In other words, we acknowledge the anthropomorphic impulse as the only epistemologically viable way we have of understanding animals, by connecting with them intellectually and emotionally, by "identifying" with them as well as identifying apparent resemblances they have with us, but at the same time remaining fully aware that such anthropomorphic projections are indeed human derived, fictions of our own desires and fears, and not necessarily the "truth" about the animal "in itself." By letting us get closer, though, to animal realities, such a self-reflective, self-critical stance works to *undo* our own anthropocentric frames of reference via an eccentric or ex-centric anthropomorphism.[22]

This book attempts to map an alternative to the forgetting, rationalization, use, and abuse of animals by humans. To forget that they exist, to put them off as if they do not count, do not have souls, or are not worthy of saving is to repeat the modern, Western denials of difference that have motivated the genocide of indigenous peoples in North America, Australia, and Africa, or the "quieter" repression of women and dissident minorities in post-Renaissance Europe and America. Refusing to see "anthropomorphic" similarities between human and other species, like refusing to see other human beings as human, is a recipe for death and destruction, not just for the victims but also for the dehumanized perpetrators, who stand to lose everything, from their own "souls" to the integrity of their natural environment. Indifference may be the prerequisite for a certain model of "objective" scientific thinking, but it has consequences whose ethical repercussions can outweigh the results of attaining the "truth." Maybe we should "*devenir animal*" first; and that means to question radically the status of our being, as well as the status of the other beings with whom we share our world.

This may be easier said than done in a contemporary climate where the animal—even the household pet!—has increasingly become an object of fear, revulsion, even primal terror and in a world where animals appear to be on the decline in terms of their day-to-day presence in human existence. A mere two or three generations ago, humans lived in intimate proximity not only with the domesticated animals every family required (horses, mules, or donkeys for transportation and field work; dogs for security; cats for rodent control; all manner of cattle for physical sustenance, including food and clothing) but even with the wild beasts that were never farther away than the nearest tree line. With the advent of modern industrialized urban society, such human-animal proximity has been increasingly reduced, and animals have been limited to serving as emotional fetishes (companion pets), as invisible mass purveyors of meat, eggs, milk, leather, hormones, and so on, or as distant aestheticized objects that are either virtually extinct (and so objects of pitiable contemplation), efficiently corralled into those vast confines known as national parks, or "preserved" in the prisonlike enclaves of zoos. When animals "mysteriously" reappear outside these tightly controlled zones, the effect is newsworthy and a source of consternation and alarm: companion animals that bite, diseases produced by the animals of industrialized farming passed on to the human food supply, bears found splashing about in suburban swimming pools, deer eating garden flowers and spreading Lyme ticks, wilderness joggers confronted by mountain lions, escaped zoo animals running amok: the list is apparently endless. And as such appearances of the animal become paradoxically more unusual as well as more common, there seems to have disappeared from human behavior any kind of common sense in dealing with animals. As the expression "horse sense" seems to have become emptied of all but metaphorical content, social workers repeatedly claim the benefit of horse farms for delinquent youth, the most hardened of whom symptomatically evince a strange dread of horses. Overcoming that fear through caring for horses can be the first step in a successful program of social reintegration. Nowhere, though, does the fear and indeed stupidity of human beings appear more prominent today than in the hysterical fear of dog bites, regularly presented by contemporary media as a danger of epidemic proportions. In her famous book *Bandit,* Vicki Hearne discusses the case of a reputedly "mean" "pitbull." Here, the quotation marks indicate terms that need to be put *sous rature.* Hearne reveals that the fictitious construct "pitbull," far from being a recognized breed of the American Kennel Club or any other canine association, is a veritable floating signifier applied to any small, terrier-like dog that exhibits aggression, especially if that untoward behavior is placed in the racialized context of poor, urban America. "Meanness," on the other hand, is a clearly anthropomorphic term that appears here to deny any anthropomorphic sympathy or inquiry by branding an animal as *innately* uncivilized (i.e., insufficiently submissive to humans) and so deserving of "termination" (i.e., death by injection). Humans are thereby relieved of the obligation to question the reasons for the dog's bad behavior, leaving it to their subordinated canine companion to pay the ultimate price for actions orchestrated either deliberately or negligently by human "owners." Finally, one cannot help but wonder how much of this hysteria is fueled by the dislodgement of the classic residents of the Renaissance domestic enclosure (women, children, pets, servants, etc.) as they refuse to remain hidden from view within its privatized space and demand to venture out into the once exclusively elite and male space of the public.

In sum, this book is about how animals intersect with our lives and how this intersection often blurs the anxiously demarcated boundary between human and animal, especially in that space, the home, that we equate with our innermost values and being. While dominant cultural norms typically interpret animal-human bonds in a negative way, I hope to show how those very bonds help us rethink the shifting boundaries of the animal and human and how an interspecies relation transforms the very core of our domestic space, perhaps even arguing for a larger notion of the family. To deconstruct the binary animal/human divide in the representation of animals and humans in texts is to try to reclaim a loss that we are always in some way mourning. Perhaps this book can testify to the reality of this mourning so as to allow the lost other of our beings to find a way into the symbolic and express a realm of meaning that has been consistently denied to animals and thus to us.[23] Texts can thus serve as an important way of rethinking animal studies through postmodern theory and deconstructing its speciesism, as well as refiguring domestic spaces to include animals—or, if one prefers, building creatural diversity.

· · ·

Textual evidence does exist of alternative visions of domestic space since at least the Middle Ages, if not even earlier, in Classical antiquity. In *Beasts and Beauties,* I examine at length the enduring cult of Diana, goddess of the hunt, and her hounds. There I propose that Diana emerges as a powerful Renaissance icon positing a communion of women and beasts.[24] The figure of Diana continues to be invoked as a powerfully affective topos that emerges across many historical times and places and haunts the literary texts of the women writers I study in this book.[25] But whereas Renaissance depictions place Diana within the patriarchal domestic enclosure or at its boundary, more modern depictions place her distinctly *outside* it. In my argument, I read how Wharton, Barnes, and Colette appropriate the myth of Diana as a figure for female empowerment and topos of female resistance, either through a literary recasting of her power over a patriarchy that would relegate women to a secondary status or as the motivating force that imaginatively redesigns a domestic space free from the patriarchal hierarchy of domestic management and instead featuring a cohabitation of various beings living harmoniously and without the fear of unnecessary subordination. Is there, one might ask, any justification for seeing such a wider, utopic fulfillment of women's community in what we know of the ancient cult of Diana/Artemis and its possible successors?[26]

One of the peculiar aspects of the Diana myth is the accumulation around the goddess not only of different but also of contradictory roles and traits: she is both ideal virgin *and* goddess of childbirth, maiden *and* mother, protector of animals *and* goddess of the hunt, safeguard of the young *and* bringer of sudden death, sensitive to the plight of even the tiniest creature yet demanding the bloodiest of sacrifices. A relatively minor figure in the Greek pantheon as it is represented in the extant literature, she was nevertheless in practice among the most worshipped of all the gods. As Carole Law Trachy has brilliantly argued, the male poets and artists who elaborated myths in their stories and images had little interest in a female deity who was primarily concerned with the women's biological processes, such as menses, fertility, and parturition. "A lack of empathy" with female experience led them to suppress these aspects of the goddess and to stress the aspect most understandable to the masculine world, that of the virgin huntress.[27] Meanwhile the female cults preserved the more complex image of a goddess who, by ruling over every phase of women's lives, from maiden to mother to crone, could be *both* the "virgin of virgins" *and* the "mother of mothers," a giver of life as well as of death (in the throes of childbirth). Obviously, a crucial deity in the daily lives of women, "the very essence of a female deity," she was not surprisingly "the most popular goddess in Greece."[28]

If, however, we return to this myth as it is read during the Renaissance, we see primarily the male fascination with the myth of Actaeon slain by his dogs after a glimpse of the goddess. The celebration of the virgin huntress in portraiture, while giving women a certain due and at least the possibility of appropriating for themselves the hitherto male world of the hunt, significantly narrowed the field of interests covered by the ancient cult of Diana as it continued subterraneously or unconsciously to be practiced in Europe: the protection and cultivation of women's bodies, of the young, and of animals. As the manifold aspects of Diana suggest, reimaginings of her story can be either joyously utopic or tragically dystopic for women and their aspirations to a domestic order of their own, undetermined by the male privilege of the *pater familias* or his avatars. In England, for example, women thought to be "witches" were burned with their "familiars," domestic pets such as cats or dogs.

. . .

My three modern "Dianas," Edith Wharton, Djuna Barnes, and Colette, revise the Diana myth to accommodate the role animals play in their sometimes radical reconfigurations of domestic space. Wharton, with her fantastical tale "Kerfol" about ghost dogs and domestic vengeance, Barnes, with the surrealist eroticism and animalism of *Nightwood,* and Colette, with her sketches and tales about life with beasts both domestic and wild, all redraw the space of home life in imaginative ways that leave the patriarchal model of a dominating *pater familias* as but one possibility among many others. These modern women writers—Diana-like—thus explode and scramble the very space of domesticity, not by abandoning it, but by imaginatively and practically reconfiguring its boundaries. Edith Wharton, author of the poem "From Artemis to Actaeon," also wrote what can only be called a dog ghost story that spins a fantastic plot of domestic revenge. In a less fantastical but more surrealist mode, Djuna Barnes uncorks the unrepentant animalism of desire in the concluding section of *Nightwood,* a fiction whose very title evokes the privileged nocturnal meeting ground of those who worship the moon goddess. Finally, Colette, presented under the figure of Diana by the poet Francis Jammes, undertook in the wake of divorcing her first husband a radical change of genre from the naughty schoolgirl novels written under his tutelage to a wide variety of animal stories, dialogues, and sketches that ultimately led her to explore the limits of domestication itself. For all three of these women writers, among many possible others, animals play a determining role in the reconfiguration of domesticity and the exploration of alternative possibilities. For these modern *streghe* (witches), the domestic ceases to be the confining site of a patriarchal arrangement and becomes a site of multivalent sexualities and polymorphous libidinal impulses whose limits remain to be charted—hence the title of this study, "Polymorphous Domesticities."

A long final chapter returns us to a male case of human-animal love and domesticity, namely the case of a pet becoming in turn a love object, if not the jealous lover, of the twentieth-century British writer J.R. Ackerley. The unpredictable effects of desire mediated through a beast give rise in this writer not only to a series of books exploring the intricacies of his relationship with a German shepherd dog named Queenie but also to a consciousness of the beast within us. His work also traces the dynamics whereby an avowedly misogynist homosexual morphs into an utter misanthrope while learning to love his bitch's "femininity." Ackerley is neither Actaeon nor Diana, and after our examination of the gynocentric spaces inspired by our three Dianas it is helpful to explore how such alternative domesticities can recross gender lines. My study of Ackerley thus completes this book because he realizes, or, better yet, incarnates, the polymorphous diversity of the ways desire can work regardless of the subjectivity of one's gender or the "choice" of love object. Homosexual desire (or same-sex object choice, to speak the language of technical psychoanalysis) within the context of this study (and including the three Dianas as well as Ackerley) is not a kind of identity formation and certainly not some kind of hard-wired "orientation," sexual being, or "lifestyle." Rather, the freedom to express same-sex desire in a heteronormative world allows for an even freer expression of cross-species desire. Inevitably, the questions raised by the polymorphous domestic relations studied here are about not the kind of object one chooses but the kind of relationship that obtains between different beings, whether humans of the same or different sex or nonhuman creatures. Of course, exploitation, cruelty, and neglect can happen—and sadly, all too frequently *do* happen—in any such relationship, but the stories examined in this book also offer positive explorations of nonconventional forms of intimacy between different creatures, and different kinds of creatures. Even what sexuality might mean in such encounters needs to be carefully unpacked, and for this reason I take the time to examine the specific eroticism of

Ackerley's love for Queenie while absolutely respecting what I find to be his thoroughly convincing defense against any potential charges of bestiality. In this case, I find the psychoanalytic tracking of how desire is cathected, decathected, and recathected especially useful in coming to a better understanding of how intersubjective processes work to sustain enduring, positive relationships, whether involving human creatures, nonhuman creatures, or both.

Thus, through the kinds of literary case studies presented here, I hope to broaden the discussion of human-animal relations beyond the traditional debates over anthropomorphism to a much more complex (and posthumanist) field of multivalent polymorphous identities, identifications, and domestic practices. As I have consistently done over the years, I take a methodological approach profoundly based in a critical appreciation of the classic psychoanalytic theory of Sigmund Freud and Jacques Lacan, tempered by a long-standing commitment to and involvement with historical work and feminist theory. As always, though, I remain wedded to a critical practice based in the close reading of specific literary texts that in turn allows for the concrete revision of theoretical paradigms. This work is no different, and the individual readings of these four writers propose in turn a more expansive model of who we are as human beings in a context where nonhuman beings have as much to tell us in a "posthumanist" world, and with as much urgency, as any of the classic thinkers or theorists.

CHAPTER I

Re-Visions of Diana in Edith Wharton

My reading of Edith Wharton's poem "Artemis to Actaeon" and her short story "Kerfol" will situate these works in the broader context of what has been called Wharton's "lurking feminism," which refigures the myth of Diana as protector of those under her care and punisher of those who would violate her sacred charges.[1] Edith Wharton's "Artemis to Actaeon" serves as an introduction to the short story "Kerfol," even though no direct narrative link exists between the two pieces. The poem shows that Wharton knew quite well the myth of Diana and Actaeon, and a more covert inscription of that myth can be found in the chilling story "Kerfol," where ghostly dogs wreak a Dianesque revenge upon a jealous and possessive husband who ends up dead with unexplainable canine bites all over his corpse. Nonetheless, his wife, Anne de Cornault, ultimately pays the price for her husband's mysterious "murder": in this tale of thwarted domesticity, she is driven mad by inexpressible grief—rendered even more poignant in the context of the cold and contemptuous treatment of her during her court trial—and a domestic space becomes her prison.

As the story begins, we read of Anne's repeated attempts to create a domestic space where she can live peacefully and joyously in the company of a small dog, a longing rendered impossible by her cruel husband. A "polymorphous domesticity" remains elusive, existing only in the trace form of a desire to enjoy the affection and loyalty of a dog in a world dominated by patriarchal power and privilege. In this revision of Dianic myth, ghostly dogs kill Yves de Cornault for his transgressions against both his wife *and* her dogs. Here Wharton plays the role of Diana herself, punishing a vicious man for harming those whom Diana would protect.

All of Wharton's ghost stories explore the status of women and men, their prescribed gender roles in society, and the fate that their sexual desires or their gender brings down upon them. As Jennifer Dyman has shown, it is within the ghost stories that a critique of social norms emerges as a corrective to patriarchy. Dyman uses the term *lurking* to describe how Wharton's feminist inclinations seem to be expressed covertly and indirectly in the spectral figures that haunt her work. Indeed, Wharton never described herself as a feminist and was leery of feminism. She came from an upper-class background and consciously took its rules of behavior seriously. When she was in her fifties she underwent a bitter divorce at a time when women had little standing and few options outside marriage. But her husband had not shared her passion for literature or creativity, nor had he been in any way sympathetic to her needs and desires, so the divorce did free her finally from marital domestic obligations. The lion's share of Wharton's work is concerned with gender issues and the oppression and loneliness of women (and men) under patriarchy. Wharton's personal unhappiness was intensified by the political upheaval of an impending World War I and the lack of any stable future. Like many of the avant-garde literati of the day, Wharton found refuge in Paris, where she took up residence. "Kerfol" and her other ghost stories are a testament to her struggles to rethink the traditional social structures of a patriarchal world that would keep women as mere objects to be possessed, neglected, and dispensed of willy-nilly, like any other domestic creature, human or nonhuman, that inhabits the patriarch's domestic enclosure and may become an inconvenience.

Wharton felt closely connected with animals, particularly dogs. They inhabited not only her poems and fiction but also her life: she was companion to several Pekingese, stylish small lapdogs very similar in type to the fashionable dogs of the Renaissance.[2] Dogs were a source of love that fostered in her a need to understand the ties she felt with them as well as the human-animal bond in general. It is not surprising, then, that the myth of Diana would appeal to her.

Yet on one occasion Wharton expressed an ambivalence about her relation to the world of animals, and especially to the world of dogs. In her diary, at age sixty-two, she wrote: "I am secretly afraid of animals—

all animals except dogs, and even some dogs. I think it is because of the *Usness* in their eyes, with the underlying *Not-Usness* which belies it, and it is so tragic a reminder of the lost age when we human beings branched off and left them to eternal inarticulateness and slavery."[3] What she reads in their eyes both reflects and deflects human beings, signals both a connection between us and them, self and other, and the individual differences that exist between all sentient beings. Perhaps the cause of fear that she suggests has to do with a tragic awareness that animals have been relegated to the status of a meaningless "other," so that the "Usness" and the "Not-Usness" in their eyes express a trauma created by "we human beings [who] branched off and left them to eternal inarticulateness"; there is a grievance in the eyes of the dogs, who in this way silently but paradoxically speak to humanity's lack of any accountability for their abjected status. Given the prominence of Cartesian thought in Wharton's day, in which animals were held to be mere automata, we can especially sympathize with her fear at seeing both the us and the not-us in their eyes. The gulf that separates us from them is written there by Western narratives of human supremacy over nature. Wharton shares with later thinkers, namely Emmanuel Levinas, Jacques Derrida, and J. M. Coetzee, the experience of seeing the "look" of the animal (Levinas) as an irrefutable call (Derrida) and as a "conversion experience" (Coetzee) that we remain dutifully bound to act upon, either though writing (literature, philosophy, critical studies) or through activism, since that look demands a long-awaited corrective against any further negation or indifference to their beings. Wharton experiences the fear or dread that such a recognition drives into the soul of a human being, who then must ask him- or herself: What does it say about us as a species that we define ourselves as intrinsically separate from the "natural" world, to which animals seem to belong though we apparently do not? At the heart of this recognition lies a trauma for human beings as well, which Wharton understands, brought on by the violent separation between human and nonhuman that has characterized Western thought and culture, and from this trauma arises, for some individuals, the felt need to defend and protect animals against a perceived gross injustice. For Wharton, this intuitive understanding of animals' position in the human order intersects with the unacknowledged feminist leanings we find throughout her work.

A second passage from Wharton shows a modern Diana-like sensibility expressed, not only as a drive to protect animals from harm and injustice, but as a drive to undo the binarism of human/animal and instead connect the self to animals in a shared creaturely status. This "polymorphous" register would imply another kind of being, "an intermediare creature" between human and animal:

> I always had a deep, instinctive understanding of animals, a yearning to hold them in my arms, a fierce desire to protect them against pain and cruelty. The feeling seemed to have its source in a curious sense of being, somehow, myself, *an intermediare creature between human beings and animals,* and nearer, on the whole, to the furry tribes than to homo sapiens. I felt I knew things about them—their sensations, desires and sensibilities—that other bipeds could not guess; and this seemed to lay on me the obligation to defend them against human oppressors. The feeling grew in intensity until it became a morbid preoccupation.[4]

Nothing more clearly demonstrates the protective and transformative role Wharton felt with regard to animals than the above passage. Some critics have read her love for dogs as a substitute for love of children. I would caution against such a reductive reading.[5] Diana was the goddess who looked after women, the young, and animals, all of them, not as entities who could substitute for each other but as a plurality of individual beings living together. A reading that would reduce the desire for the company of animals to a mere a stand-in for the desire to have a child is dismantled in Wharton's own words. She clearly understands her "curious sense of being . . . an *intermediare* creature," closer in affect and being to the "furry tribes" than to "homo sapiens," as transformative of her human nature.

. . .

Wharton's "Artemis to Actaeon" (1909) is, as the title indicates, a long prosopopoeia where the goddess both declares her love and explains her divine point of view to an apparently uncomprehending Actaeon.[6] Encouraging and justifying his action by way of an erotics of transgression, or rather an extreme form of *carpe diem* where one brief moment of ecstasy outweighs a life that is long and secure but deathly monotonous, Artemis explicates the beauty of Actaeon's awful end, in which he is mauled to death by his own hounds upon having beheld her in her bath. The gods' drab, unending immortality is actually a kind of death in which "they pale, for lack of warmth they wane, / Freeze to the marble of their images." For ". . . immortality is not to range / Unlimited through vast Olympian days, / Or sit in dull dominion over time." When a "rash votary" like Actaeon fatally glimpses forbidden divinity, his act "renews" the gods; their "incarnation," and thus continuing life, depends upon the impassioned desire of a human being to come close to them, while their oblivion is sealed by human apathy.

The position of the gods, then, is the erotic one of passivity, a sense of being alive only when one *becomes* the love object of some worthy other. This is the position traditionally ascribed by Freud to femininity. By redefining it as that of the gods, "who are but what you [mortals] make us," Wharton not only dignifies what psychoanalysis views as an inferior position but more importantly places the emphasis most strenuously on the *worthiness* of the human lover. The gods are not interested in just any worshipper. In fact, the reverential and respectful ones who duly leave their prescribed sacrificial offerings are most certainly not the ones who awaken the gods out of their doldrums. Neither are those immature ones who break into the most sacred loci of their being but then, unappreciatively, "to their incurious loves return." In a passage reminiscent of Giordano Bruno's Neo-Platonic revision of the Actaeon myth, only a select few, whose glimpse of godliness means they can never return to their previous existences, are worthy of having their love reciprocated by the gods, whose act of love is also an act of death:

> Not so with thee; for some indeed there are
> Who would behold the truth and then return
> To pine among the semblances—but I
> Divined in thee the questing foot that never
> Revisits the cold hearth of yesterday
> Or calls achievement home. I from afar
> Beheld thee fashioned for one hour's high use,
> Nor meant to slake oblivion drop by drop.
> Long, long hadst thou inhabited my dreams,
> Surprising me as harts surprise a pool,
> Stealing to drink at midnight; I divined
> Thee rash to reach the heart of life, and lie
> Bosom to bosom in occasion's arms,
> And said: *Because I love thee thou shalt die!* [emphasis in text]

Only the Actaeons are worthy of love by the gods, whose dreams they already "inhabit" in their transformed essences as "harts" who "surprise a pool." Only they whom the gods perceive as "rash to reach the heart of life" are worthy of that fatal embrace that allows them to achieve true immortality, which is "to drink fate's utmost at a draught" rather than "feel the wine grow stale upon the lip." By losing himself in her, Actaeon "relives" in the "renewal" of Artemis, thus binding their fates forever. He is, then, a most worthy lover of the deity, and the only question that remains—a terribly important one and the one that in fact generates the poem—is whether Actaeon understands all this or not. The whole text thus rests on a conundrum whereby the erotic power of transgression so extolled by the poem may not be known by the one whose consequent apotheosis is being celebrated. Eros may preclude its own cognition. Actaeon may never know that Artemis indeed *wanted* him to startle her in the privacy of her bath, to undergo his beastly and fatal transformation as the true path to immortality and closeness to god.

Very different from this positive framing of Actaeon's death from the vantage point of Artemis is the fantastic tale of "Kerfol," where death by dogs is hardly the attainment of a blissful union. Originally published in 1916 at the height of the First World War while Wharton was living in France, "Kerfol" describes strange events that purportedly took place at a Breton castle in the seventeenth century. Those events are presented within a frame narration set in modern times and told in the first person. The narrator, who confesses to having "always had secret yearnings for domesticity" despite an "unsociable exterior," has been encouraged by a friend to buy an old estate in Brittany: "just the place for a solitary-minded devil like you."[7] "Buyer beware" is of course the immediate connotation of this situation, even if the warning were not already phonetically evident from the story's title and name of the castle: Kerfol or careful! Suspicions are heightened when the narrator's attempt to visit the castle is thwarted by the absence of the guardian and the strange presence of a motley group of dogs, a "cloud of witnesses" (213) who observe the narrator attentively and silently while maintaining their distance. The silence and lack of commotion are, of course, signs that things are not as they seem: "as though the silence of the place had gradually benumbed their busy inquisitive natures. And this strange passivity, this almost human lassitude, seemed to me sadder than the misery of starved and beaten animals" (214). Curiously, the pathos of the animals is a function of their apparent "humanness." At the same time, though, the narrator describes a tremendous feeling of "remoteness" from them, which ultimately leads to the thought that they have "in common one memory so deep and dark that nothing that had happened since was worth either a growl or a wag" (214)—some alien, incommunicable secret or trauma such that the gap between the narrator and these creatures, who appear to be the sole residents of the manor, appears radically unbridgeable. The narrator concludes—and loudly announces to the assembly of dogs—that they look as if they had seen a ghost and wonders aloud if there might not be some ghost haunting Kerfol. The reader is even led to wonder if the existence of such a ghost is what is prompting the eagerness of its owners to sell the property "for a song."

Only upon returning to the friend's home, with the feeling of "having escaped from the loneliest place in the world, and of not liking loneliness," does the narrator learn that the dogs seen there earlier are themselves the ghosts of Kerfol, rumored to congregate and appear there on a certain day during the year. With ratiocinative impulses aroused as any property-buying desires have receded, the narrator eventually finds an "explanation" for the ghost dogs in the story that provides the embedded narrative by way of the court record of a seventeenth-century murder trial. In accordance with the early modern tradition of the found manuscript, the record is said to have been edited into "a simpler form," the narrator claiming, of course, that "nowhere have I added anything of my own" (216). The embedded narrative relates the dolorous tale of one Anne de Cornault, accused of having murdered her husband, Yves de Cornault, lord of Kerfol, with the help of an accomplice/lover, Hervé de Lanrivain (a distant ancestor of the narrator's friend who uncannily bears the exact same name). The setting, period, and outline of the plot are highly reminiscent of the Renaissance novella, and except for the fantastic conclusion the story could easily pass for a tale by Marguerite de Navarre: an unhappy, aristocratic marriage between a jealous husband and lonely wife in a deserted location ("the loneliest place in the world") leads the wife to take a local lover until the husband's discovery of the affair, which brings about a gruesome denouement that leaves the principals dead or mad. Between fits of lunacy, Anne herself is put on trial for the murder—until finally the judges have no choice but to commit her back to the care of her husband's family, who lock her in the keep at Kerfol till her dying day. Yet the physical evidence surrounding Yves's death is inconclusive and puzzling: "He had been dreadfully scratched and gashed about the face and throat, as if with curious pointed weapons; and one of his legs had a deep tear in it which had cut an artery, and probably caused his death" (219).

Vigorously protesting her innocence, Anne takes the stand in her own defense with a tale so unbelievable that her own lawyer tries unsuccessfully to dissuade her from recounting it. Here is where the mysterious dogs enter the picture and also where Wharton's story radically departs from its early modern models. According to Anne's testimony, her husband turns out to be nothing less than a canocidal Bluebeard whose ultimate demise is as implausible as it is poetically just. A fiercely jealous man, often away on business trips, Yves refuses to let his wife leave the castle grounds or even walk about in them unattended. Mindful that this is "the loneliest place in the world," we are not surprised to learn of Anne's terrible unhappiness, only partially palliated by the exotic and expensive gifts her husband brings back with him from his travels, including an especially prized bracelet or "necklet" of emerald, pearls, and rubies.

Yves does, however, bring back something even more endearing for his wife, something capable of making her forget all about her loneliness, "something even odder and prettier than the bracelet" (218)—a little brown dog identified elsewhere in the narrative as a rare Chinese breed known as a "Sleevedog" (212):

> "Oh, it looks like a bird or a butterfly!" she cried as she picked it up; and the dog put its paws on her shoulders and looked at her with eyes "like a Christian's." After that she would never have it out of her sight, and petted and talked to it *as if it had been a child—as indeed it was the nearest thing to a child she was to know.* Yves de Cornault was much pleased with his purchase. The dog had been brought to him by a sailor from an East India merchantman, and the sailor had bought it of a pilgrim in a bazaar at Jaffa, who had stolen it from a nobleman's wife in China: a perfectly permissible thing to do, since the pilgrim was a Christian and the nobleman a heathen doomed to hell-fire. Yves de Cornault had paid a long price for the dog, for they were beginning to be in demand at the French court, and the sailor knew he had got hold of a good thing; but Anne's pleasure was so great that, to see her laugh and play with the little animal, her husband would doubtless have given twice the sum. (218–19; emphasis added)

What is striking and foreboding about this passage, despite the mitigating final clause, is the absolute difference of affect between husband and wife, marvelously highlighted by Wharton's skillful use of both direct and free indirect style. Yves sees the dog primarily from a commodity standpoint, as a more lively and exotic version of the bejeweled bracelet. The purchase of the dog, despite its price, is a "good deal," since such dogs are "in demand" at court and probably could be sold for even more than he paid the sailor, who had bought it from a pilgrim in Jaffa, who had in turn stolen it from a Chinese aristocrat's wife. The forcible expropriation of exotic merchandise is legitimized by the non-Christian status of the Chinese *nobleman*, as if the dog's value to that nobleman's *wife* were immaterial. In fact, the patriarchal disequilibrium between husband and wife, where it is possible to steal only from the husband because he legally owns all of the property, including hers, mirrors the disequilibrium of affect between their Breton counterparts. For commodity value is the farthest thing from Anne's mind as she jubilantly greets her puppy "as if it had been a child." For Anne, the dog is literally priceless since that creature is really a fellow member of her domestic abode, a part of the family, like a child. One imagines that the Chinese nobleman's wife at the opposite end of the globe felt the same way.

The difference of views between Yves and Anne concerning the little brown dog is so extreme there is no possibility of communication between them. Only the evocation of death raises the conflict to a conscious level:

> One day she had fallen asleep in her room, with the dog at her feet, as his habit was. Her feet were bare and resting on his back. Suddenly she was waked by her husband: he stood beside her, smiling not unkindly.
> "You look like my great-grandmother, Julianne de Cornault, lying in the chapel with her feet on a little dog," he said.
> The analogy sent a chill through her, but she laughed and answered: "Well, when I am dead you must put me beside her, carved in marble, with my dog at my feet."
> "Oho—we'll wait and see," he said, laughing also, but with his black brows close together. "The dog is the emblem of fidelity."
> "And do you doubt my right to lie with mine at my feet?"
> "When I'm in doubt I find out," he answered. "I am an old man," he added, "and people say I make you lead a lonely life. But I swear you shall have your monument if you earn it."
> "And I swear to be faithful," she returned, "if only for the sake of having my little dog at my feet." (221–22)

The difference could not be more extreme. Yves's view of his wife sleeping with the little dog at her feet brings him to aestheticize her not, as he very well might, by analogy with Titian's *Venus of Urbino,* in which a voluptuous *bella* reclines on a bed with a dog at her feet, but as the sculpture on his great-grandmother's tomb. Not as life, but as death! No wonder Anne feels a "chill through her." To her nonetheless lighthearted attempt to respond by requesting to be entombed similarly, next to his ancestor but with her own little dog, he equivocates before spouting the banality about the dog as "the emblem of fidelity." Dire equivocation ensues as it becomes unclear who is supposed to be faithful to whom. If the dog is the emblem of fidelity to its master, then assuredly it deserves its place in their common tomb. If the dog is an emblem of a wife's fidelity to her spouse, then the reward for her fidelity is the funerary architecture of the tomb. If the dog is an emblem of fidelity, is that not because it is by nature faithful and therefore deserving of its master's loyalty to it? The differend here concerns whether fidelity is something to be earned (Yves's point of view) or something to be given (Anne's view). Further complicating the issue is that for Yves fidelity is what someone else owes you, while for Anne it is something you give to someone else. Yves never swears fidelity to Anne but expects that she should do so for him. Anne swears fidelity to Yves in response to his threat/incentive, but only because of an even deeper fundamental loyalty to her dog: "And I swear to be faithful, . . . if only for the sake of having my little dog at my feet." But if swearing fidelity to Yves is only a way to express and protect a more fundamental loyalty to her dog, then is she not in swearing fidelity to Yves being already unfaithful to him? And finally, in sleeping at Anne's feet, is not the dog already expressing a boundless fidelity, even as we shall see, beyond the grave? Would not Yves have every right to be jealous, then, of the dog's unquestioning loyalty (as opposed to his own relentless suspiciousness)? Or jealous, too, of his wife's greater faithfulness to her dog than to him?

All is in place for the terrible events that follow. Anne finally meets a potential lover in the shape of Hervé de Lanrivain. After a few fleeting encounters, he asks for a keepsake, as he is about to leave on a long journey. All she has to give him is the expensive bracelet, which has in the meantime been used as her dog's collar. Yves's jealous suspicions are aroused when he remarks upon the bracelet missing from the dog's neck. He says nothing to Anne, but after mysteriously recovering the bracelet he strangles the dog with it and leaves both on his wife's bed pillow. The same day Yves "had a peasant hanged for stealing a faggot in the park, and the next day he nearly beat to death a young horse he was breaking" (223). A sequence of dogs then come into Anne's life, only for each to be mysteriously strangled and deposited on the bed pillow after the slightest affection she shows them. Eventually, Anne comes to fear for her own life, as her sanity is threatened by this systematic assault on her attempts to break out of her loneliness in even the most minimal way.

One night, returning from his long absence, Hervé wishes to see Anne. Fearing for his life as well as hers, Anne goes down to the castle door to urge him away. Just then, she hears her "husband's voice calling out [her] name and cursing [her]" at the top of the stairs, followed by "a terrible scream and fall," and the sound of "dogs snarling and panting" (226). She hears Yves cry out, moan, and fall silent, then something else: "a sound like the noise of a pack when the wolf is thrown to them—gulping and lapping" (227). Pressed by the judge regarding where these dogs could have come from, since none had been sighted on the premises at Kerfol for months, she admits that she recognized them by their barking to be her "dead dogs." Though the medical evidence bears out the claim that the cuts on the victim's corpse were indeed bite marks, Anne's final response leaves the courtroom in an uproar. Charges of witchcraft are leveled at her before she is finally determined to be just "a harmless madwoman" (228). Meanwhile, the exact circumstances of Yves's demise remain unclear, and Wharton maintains the fantastical quality of the tale by *not* providing a scientific or rational alternative to the conclusion that the master of Kerfol was killed by the ghostly pack of dogs.

...

What is clear is the transitory status of the human lover, Hervé, since it is his momentous if momentary intrusion into the life at Kerfol that reorients the potential objects of Yves's jealous rage from potential human suitors to canine rivals for his wife's affections. Rather than the pet serving as an ambiguous mediator/obstacle between lover and beloved, or the concomitant possibility of desire sliding from human object to animal, we here have violence directed against the pet in the place of the human rival. The link between the two is that most prized of commodities, the bracelet, which evinces a remarkable capacity to change hands in this story: from Chinese nobleman and his wife to pilgrim to sailor to Yves to Anne to her dog to Hervé somehow back to Yves, maliciously back to the dog, and then back to Anne, who takes it and hides it in her bosom. It then somehow resurfaces as an exhibit at her trial, where it "appears to have struck the Judges and the public as a curious and valuable jewel" (218). In giving away the bracelet (or "necklet"), Anne patently demonstrates her greater love for the dog than for the expensive gift of jewelry, putting it back into exchange and willing to give away to someone else the gift that means the most to its giver. The gift, moreover, whether we understand it as bracelet or necklet, is also a mark of the recipient's possession by the giver, that is, of Anne herself as Yves's "treasure" (221) and most prized possession, the crown jewel of his domain of Kerfol. For him, the sign of her apparent infidelity means the death of "the emblem of fidelity," the dog who would have found his likeness at the stone feet of his mistress's tomb. Now that Anne has failed to "earn" her death monument for her lack of fidelity in Yves's commercialized concept of it, her dog, and indeed *any* dog that comes into her space, must also die, since it is not just her dog but "*the* dog" that "is the emblem of fidelity." Hence, the symbolic act of reversing the funerary arrangement by depositing the strangled dogs on the pillow or headrest of Anne's bed rather than at its foot.

But this would mean Yves falls into an obsessive and impossible attempt to kill a symbol: not the flesh and blood dog but what it represents. The trouble is, all he can do is to kill the material representation, the body of the pet but not what it stands for. Ironically, his death comes about by the uncanny return of the dogs in the immaterial form of ghosts. By this return, they most aggressively reassert the validity of their emblematic association, representing fidelity itself as they return from beyond the grave to protect and avenge their mistress in her moment of greatest need. That is, they return when Yves is preparing to kill not an emblem but the person of his wife. This in turn allows the dogs to return as the "emblem of fidelity," protecting their mistress by killing her tormentor, gnawing and tearing him to bits. It will probably be obvious to the reader by now that the name *Anne* is also a derivative of *Di-anne*, but in this version of the story the dogs belong not to Actaeon but to the goddess whose intimacy he would violate. Or, perhaps, to revise the myth, they were Diana's hounds all along and never did belong to Actaeon except in his presumption of ownership. Slaying him, they were not so much disloyal to him as ever faithful to their divine mistress.

Having literalized the emblem of fidelity, then, the dogs of Kerfol keep returning faithfully to haunt the castle once a year, ghostly guardians as they silently gaze. Hence, too, they uncannily appear to the narrator on her visit as both strange and familiar, as both "almost human" and incomprehensibly "remote." *Unheimlich* they certainly are in Freud's sense, being both of the home and not of the home: the ghost dogs guard an empty home that has no masters. But if they "seemed to have the place to themselves" (215), giving rise to the feeling of the uncanny, it is because the home they haunt has ceased to be a "homey" place. More exactly, their current presence in the home is the uncanny sign of their violently enforced absence from it: their murderous eviction from the *domus* by a vengeful *pater familias*. Never fully allowed into the domestic space of the home, they paradoxically can never seem to leave it. Perhaps this is why the domestic animal gone wild is so compelling as a marker of the *unheimlich*, whether stray dog, or black cat, or excessively proximate bird of prey. As the emblem of fidelity, the ghost dogs of Kerfol remain the ineffaceable sign of a troubled domesticity. As such, these creatures—properly belonging neither inside nor outside the home—can attain no more than the ghostly existence of a semblance: the semblance of children to Anne, the semblance of rival lovers to Yves, the semblance of owners to the narrator. The sign of something they are not, they are also by this negativity the constant reminder of the home that is not.

Such is, of course, the familiar if tragic world of Wharton's major fiction: the unrealized dream of Actaeon in all its erotic transcendence countermanded by the harsh reality of the patriarchal household inhabited only by the ghost of that dream. Is there any reason for surprise that it is not in her realist fiction but in her ghost stories that we find the strongest assertions of Wharton's "lurking feminism"? As Gilbert and Gubar note, the supernatural tale epitomized by "Kerfol" provided a literary alternative to "the bleak skepticism that kept her from fantasizing . . . about changes in sex roles and social rules," namely a way of "simultaneously saying the unsayable and enacting its unsayability" with regard to the oppressiveness of the patriarchal order. Gilbert and Gubar argue that the ghost story "consistently made possible just the transgressive protest against 'reality' that she secretly longed to mount": on the one hand "the unleashing of female rage as well as the release of female desire" and on the other hand "the expression of female pain at the repression of rage and the killing of desire." Any of those "secret yearnings for domesticity" fleetingly evoked in "Kerfol" would appear, then, to be realized only in negative form, emblematized once more by the very muteness of the ghost dogs, saying what cannot be said.

As for Wharton herself, she neither suffered in silence nor waited for a supernatural revenge but resolutely and courageously broke the mold in the practice of her life (far more than most of her critics have given her credit for). She divorced her only husband at age fifty-one after moving to France, where she lived by herself, keeping a literary salon and Pekingese dogs, until her death in 1937.

BEASTLY BECOMINGS IN DJUNA BARNES'S *NIGHTWOOD*

The year of Edith Wharton's death, 1937, saw the publication by another American expatriate of a strange novel whose wild alternative to the traditional domestic order also references the beast in general and the dog in particular: *Nightwood*, by Djuna Barnes. If Edith Wharton characterizes her position with regard to the world of animals as an intermediary place between the human and the nonhuman and admits feeling closer to the "furry tribes," Djuna Barnes crafts a relation to the inhuman in *Nightwood*, through the figure of Robin, that can also be described as a tertiary position, a polyvalent space that undoes binary distinctions, symbolized in my readings as the quest for a polymorphous domesticity. Indeed, the underlying "wildness" found both in Wharton's short story "Kerfol" and in Barnes's *Nightwood* leads us to what Teresa de Lauretis has called "a psychic space haunted by the muted phantasms of a past both individual and collective."[8] In other words, these phantasms, whether they emerge as avenging dogs (Kerfol) or as both beast and dog (*Nightwood*), are figures summoned by an "excess of affect" that cannot (will not!) be tamed by normative domestic enclosures.[9]

In her meticulous reading of Freud's notion of drive, especially with regard to Djuna Barnes's *Nightwood,* de Lauretis argues for affect as a pure drive that "straddles the divide between animal and human, and partaking of both, . . . inhabits a borderland between the somatic and the mental capacity for representation, a 'borderland' that is the psyche itself."[10] More than the mediator of desire, the beast in *Nightwood* is a powerful transformer of social, sexual, and psychical identity. And if any character in this tale of transvestite doctors, incestuous grandmothers, and neurasthenic aristocrats incarnates the transience of identity, it is Robin Vote. Robin is that beast, figured as what de Lauretis describes as "an excess of affect or unbound psychic energy . . . a figure of sexuality as an *undomesticated, unsymbolizable* force" (emphasis mine).[11]

A character in constant flight like the bird signaled by her first name, Robin pulls the plot along with her as she hops from home to home and relationship to relationship: from Felix to Nora to Jenny and back to Nora. *Unheimlich* to the core, as it were, she is both obsessively "haunted" by the "wish for a home" and completely incapable of staying there when she finds one.[12] Inhabited by a "tragic longing to be kept, knowing herself astray" (74), Robin nonetheless cannot be kept. She comes and goes as she pleases, eventually leaving her lovers in complete despair. "I don't want to be here," she says symptomatically upon first meeting Nora (70), foreshadowing the stormy vicissitudes of their relationship. Robin's *wanderlust* is also at the same time what defines her as everyone's elusive object of desire, much like Ariosto's beloved Angelica.

At the same time, Robin's fidgety relation to the domestic—her wild side, so to speak—interfaces with her evident transsexuality (she is "a tall girl with the body of a boy" [58], wearing "boy's trousers" [210]) and apparent animality. We first see her at the Hôtel Récamier, lying in a swoon witnessed by the *chasseur* of the hotel, the doctor who has been summoned to aid her, and the doctor's friend Baron Felix. She is a highly aestheticized beast:

> Like a painting by the *douanier* Rousseau, [Robin] seemed to lie in a *jungle trapped in a drawing room.* . . . The woman who presents herself to the spectator as a "picture" forever arranged is, for the contemplative mind, the chiefest danger. Sometimes one meets *a woman who is beast turning human.* Such a person's every movement will reduce to an image of a forgotten experience; a mirage of an eternal wedding cast on the racial memory; as insupportable a joy as would be the vision of an eland coming down an aisle of trees, chapleted with orange blossoms and bridal veil, a hoof raised in the economy of fear, stepping in the trepidation of flesh that will become myth; as the unicorn is neither man nor beast deprived, but human hunger pressing its breast to its prey.
>
> Such a woman is the infected carrier of the past: before her the structure of our head and jaws ache—we feel that we could eat her, she who is eaten death returning, for only then do we put our face close to the blood on the lips of our forefathers. (44–47; emphasis added)

Faced with this dangerously perfect "picture" of woman as beast, the hapless Felix falls in love with Robin, marries her, and has a child by her, only to have her leave him. The bearer of some immemorial past, infecting "us" with some unspeakable, carnivorous desire that is also the repressed truth of "our forefathers," Robin confronts us with the beasts we once were and, somewhere deep down within us, still are. It would thus seem that she is less "beast turning human," or even a beast turned toward the human, than the human turning (or returning to being) beast. Felix's error is to try ineffectually to tame her, to domesticate her within the bounds of the home and according to the traditions of his old aristocratic heritage and pedigree. But Robin as a principle is precisely what resists domestication of any kind, as undomesticatable as the wild eland or mythical unicorn. Though Felix's first sight of her raises visions of a creature walking down the aisle in bridal finery, and though she does indeed become his wife, she irrepressibly returns to that long-lost home that is our animal ancestry, "carr[ying] the quality of the 'way back' as animals do" (51–52).

When next we see her, she is at a circus, where she attracts the attention of the woman who will become her next lover, Nora Flood, by the strange reaction of the circus animals to Robin's presence. These animals, horses, "tiny" dogs "trying to look like horses," elephants, and lions, "going around and around the ring, all but climbed over at that point" where they encountered the former baroness: "Then as one powerful lioness came to the turn of the bars, exactly opposite the girl, she turned her furious great head with its yellow eyes afire and went down, her paws thrust through the bars and, as she regarded the girl, as if a river were falling behind impossible heat, her eyes flowed in tears that never reached the surface" (69–70). Confronted by this conspicuous display of the animals' desire, as if she were infecting them with the same longings that the human beings who saw her in the Paris hotel experienced, Robin asks Nora to help her leave, so beginning their love affair. Nora represents a highly unconventional domesticity, living alone with her hound on the edge of civilization yet running "the strangest 'salon' in America":

> Her house was couched in the centre of a mass of tangled grass and weeds. Before it fell into Nora's hands the property had been in the same family two hundred years. It had its own burial ground, and a decaying chapel in which stood in tens and tens mouldering psalm books, laid down some fifty years gone in a flurry of forgiveness and absolution.
> It was the "paupers" salon for poets, radicals, beggars, artists, and people in love; for Catholics, Protestants, Brahmins, dabblers in black magic and medicine; all these could be seen sitting about her oak table before the huge fire, Nora listening, her hand on her hound, the firelight throwing her shadow and his high against the wall. Of all that ranting, roaring crew, she alone stood out. (64)

Like a New World Diana in her sylvan abode, Nora installs herself in the zone between nature and culture, animal and human, sacred and profane, eroticism and death: "She was one of those deviations by which man thinks to reconstruct himself" (68). Her main fault is her generosity by which she "robbed herself for everyone . . . continually turning about to find herself diminished" (66). For a "wild thing caught in a woman's skin" (182) like Robin, Nora is the closest thing to home and the one she ultimately returns to after her unrestrained wanderings, including the long detour of her affair with Jenny. Perhaps this is because, unlike everyone else who desires Robin as an object to hold and to possess, Nora is the only one whose love for Robin is motivated out of generosity: she is the one who saves her from the circus of others' carnivorous desires, be they human or animal!

Jenny Petherbridge is Nora Flood's opposite and beastly in ways only a human could be: a wealthy, middle-aged widow who "had been like a squirrel racing a wheel day and night in an endeavor to make [each of four now dead husbands] historical; they could not survive it" (83). Named "the squatter," this emotional pack-rat of a woman lives an utterly borrowed existence, desperately living off the words, deeds, and emotions of others, a hollow individual in a mad search for some kind of authenticity that produces only inauthenticity: "She defiled the very meaning of personality in her passion to be a person; somewhere about her was the tension of the accident that made the beast the human endeavor.... She wanted to be the reason for everything and so was the cause of nothing" (86). As opposed to the human beast that is Robin, Jenny is a beastly human, rapacious in her appropriation of Nora's love for Robin (since theirs was "the most passionate love that she knew" [87]), a love she seals or steals by the bloody beating she gives Robin in her carriage, after which they leave together for America.

Ironically, it is such "beastly" behavior that makes Jenny the least able to understand the beast in Robin. As she complains to a commiserating Felix, "She always lets her pets die. She is so fond of them, and then she neglects them, the way that animals neglect themselves" (144). In other words, Robin neither can be domesticated nor can responsibly undertake the domestication of others. She can neither keep pets nor be a pet, especially not for Ms. Pet-her-bridge. Her only hope, it would seem, if she can face up to it, is some utterly unspeakable and primordial communion with the beasts. The final chapter of *Nightwood,* "The Possessed," dramatizes just such an encounter.

The chapter begins by evoking the familiar return of Robin's *wanderlust,* her never-ending quest for a home but absolute intolerance for staying at home, however loosely it may be defined:

> When Robin, accompanied by Jenny Petherbridge, arrived in New York, she seemed distracted. She would not listen to Jenny's suggestion that they should make their home in the country. She said a hotel was "good enough." Jenny could do nothing with her; it was as if the motive power which had directed Robin's life, her day as well as her night, had been crippled. For the first week or two, she would not go out, then, thinking herself alone, she began to haunt the terminals, taking trains into different parts of the country, wandering without design, going into many out-of-the-way churches, sitting in the darkest corner or standing against the wall. (207)

As her quest reveals a sacred dimension, she oddly assumes the persona of the domesticity that her wandering rejects, "moving like a housewife come to set straight disorder in an unknown house" (208). This paradoxical housewife in a strange house reveals once again her closeness to the animal: "Robin walked the open country in the same manner, pulling at the flowers, speaking in a low voice to the animals. Those that came near, she grasped, straining their fur back until their eyes were narrowed and their teeth bare, her own teeth showing as if her hand were upon her own neck" (208). Baring their teeth as she bares her own—a physiological display of animal aggression that is also the repressed origin of the human smile—Robin reveals her identification *with* and identity *as* a beast. At home only with the beasts, she renders the uncomprehending Jenny "hysterical," causing her to accuse Robin of a "sensuous communion with unclean spirits": "She did not understand anything Robin felt or did, which was more unendurable than her absence" (208). For Jenny, Robin's intolerably incomprehensible behavior (wandering in the countryside, visiting abandoned chapels, and engaging in dialogue with animals) can be explained only in the canonical Western terms of demon possession, witchcraft, wildness, and unspeakable perversities. No longer in Jenny's possession, Robin appears "possessed," as the chapter title indicates, whereas in fact she has stepped back out of the familiar domesticity championed in their different ways by both Jenny and Felix and into that other, counterdomestic world linked to the realm of Diana.

Robin is accordingly led back to the Dianesque figure Nora and into a landscape that resembles the ponds and bowers associated with the goddess: "Robin now headed up into Nora's part of the country. She circled closer and closer. Sometimes she slept in the woods; the silence that she had caused by her coming was broken again by insect and bird flowing back over her intrusion, which was forgotten in her fixed stillness, obliterating her as a drop of water is made anonymous by the pond into which it has fallen" (209). Unlike Actaeon, who brazenly intrudes into the world of the woods, Robin finds herself absorbed in it, disappearing into it and losing herself there like a drop of water fallen into a pool. Coming so close as to sleep in the old, run-down chapel behind Nora's house, she is awoken one night by the sound of Nora's dog barking. At this point, the narrative point of view switches to that of Nora, who becomes the privileged observer of all that subsequently happens and who reacts presciently to her dog's odd behavior, the sole cause of which can only be the proximity of Robin: "The dog was running about the house; she heard him first on one side, then the other; he whined as he ran; barking and whining she heard him farther and farther away. Nora bent forward, listening; she began to shiver" (209).

Following her dog into the pitch darkness, up the hill and through thick briars, Nora finally bursts through the chapel door to come upon her prodigal lover: "On a contrived altar, before a Madonna, two candles were burning. Their light fell across the floor and the dusty benches. Before the image lay flowers and toys. Standing before them in her boy's trousers was Robin" (210). Displayed in her transgendered (male/female), transgenerational (adult/child), and trans-species (human/beast) being, Robin is caught in an intimate act of adulation before an image of the Virgin Mother, perhaps an avatar of ancient Diana herself, but for certain a repeated figure of Robin's love for Nora, both in her affection for Nora and in the need to keep distance. As Doctor Matthew earlier explains to Nora, Robin "put you cleverly away by making you the Madonna" (183). Only later, while frantically searching for Robin in Naples, does Nora realize the import of these words. There she comes upon the sight of a girl that presages the nocturnal discovery of Robin in her chapel:

> In open door-ways night-lights were burning all day before gaudy prints of the Virgin. In one room that lay open to the alley, before a bed covered with a cheap heavy satin comforter, in the semi-darkness, a young girl sat on a chair, leaning over its back, one arm across it, the other hanging at her side, as if half of her slept, and half of her suffered. When she saw me she laughed, as children do, in embarrassment. Looking from her to the Madonna behind the candles, I knew that the image, to her, was what I had been to Robin, not a saint at all, but a fixed dismay, the space between the human and the holy head, the arena of the "indecent" eternal. At that moment I stood in the centre of eroticism and death, . . . , and I knew in that bed Robin should have put me down. (196)

To be someone else's "Madonna" is not only about being honored with churchgoing reverence usually reserved for holy saints, it is also to become a figure of transition to a place beyond where human and sacred, virginal and maternal are dramatically drawn together. The imago of the female deity, Mary or Diana, is a source of fascination and fear, of joy and suffering, of ecstasy and transgression, that recalls both a "primitive innocence" and the "'indecent' eternal." Such is the understanding Nora finally reaches about the nature of her relationship with Robin: "It was *me* made her hair stand on end because I loved her. She turned bitter because I made her fate colossal. . . . So the lover must go against nature to find love" (194; emphasis in text). A primary figure of this antinatural love is that of incest, and it is incarnated by Nora's beloved: "For Robin is incest too; that is one of her powers. . . . Yet not being [of] the family she is more present than the family. A relative is in the foreground only when it is born, when it suffers and when it dies, unless it becomes one's lover, then it must be everything, as Robin was" (195). The transgressiveness foregrounded here is highly reminiscent of Georges Bataille's famous theories about the relation between death and eroticism, which were circulating in the

1930s Paris inhabited by Djuna Barnes.[13] Yet Robin's attraction to the eroticism of transgression is ambiguous, since in her case the "indecent eternal" must cohabit with a primitive sense of innocence. Only Nora, as Felix acknowledges, can supply Robin with this apparently contradictory need: "[Robin] always seemed to be looking for someone to tell her that she was innocent . . . always searching in the wrong direction until she met Nora Flood. . . . There are some people . . . who must get permission to live, and if the Baronin [Robin] finds no one to give her that permission, she will make an innocence for herself; a fearful sort of primitive innocence. It may be considered 'depraved' by our generation, but our generation does not know everything" (147). Holding Nora in a kind of "fixed dismay," Robin both desires and flees her until she ultimately comes "home" to her at the end of the novel, a home to which Nora has returned after her revelation in Naples.

It is there, at the end, in Nora's chapel, before her makeshift altar to the Madonna, that Robin is free to indulge in a final, cathartic act of primitive innocence/indecency in beastly communion with Nora's dog and under the watchful eye of the virgin mother, Nora/Diana. Here, then, is the final scene of *Nightwood,* a scene of demonstrably "wild" domesticity that Nora observes without being a participant after she bursts through the chapel door:

> Robin began going down. Sliding down she went; her hair swinging, her arms held out, and the dog stood there rearing back, his forelegs slanting; his paws trembling under the trembling of his rump, his hackle about his neck standing out stiff and beautiful, his mouth open, the tongue slung sideways over his sharp bright teeth; whining and waiting. And down she went, until her head swung against his; on all fours now, dragging her knees. The veins stood out in her neck, under her ears, swelled in her arms, and wide and throbbing rose up on her fingers as she moved forward.
>
> The dog, quivering in every muscle, sprang back, his lips drawn, his tongue a stiff curving terror in his mouth; moved backward, back, as she came on, whimpering too now, coming forward, her head turned completely sideways, grinning and whimpering. Backed now into the farthest corner, the dog reared as if to avoid something that troubled him to such agony that he seemed to be rising from the floor; then he stopped, clawing sideways at the wall, his forepaws lifted and sliding, looking at her, striking against the wall, like a little horse; like something imploring a bird. Then as she, now head down, dragging her forelocks in the dust, struck against his side, he let loose one howl of misery and bit at her, dashing about her, barking, and as he sprang on either side of her he always kept his head toward her, dashing his rump now this side, now that, of the wall.

> Then she began to bark also, crawling after him—barking in a fit of laughter, obscene and touching. The dog began to cry then, running with her, head-on with her head, as if slowly and surely to circumvent her; soft and slow his feet went padding. He ran this way and that, low down in his throat crying, and she grinning and crying with him; crying in shorter and shorter spaces, moving head to head, until she gave up, lying out, her hands beside her, her face turned and weeping; and the dog too gave up then, and lay down, his eyes bloodshot, his head flat along her knees. (210-11)

Falling to her hands and knees in the wake of Nora's intrusion, Robin interacts with her four-legged companion, on an equal footing with him, so to speak, brought down to his level of beastliness—or, alternatively, finally allowed to be the self that others (both human and animal) have recognized her to be, namely that of "a beast turning human," by in turn becoming a human turning beast. Dog and girl interact in an escalating spiral of mimicry and reciprocal motion, whose physicality, emotional intensity, and tempo leave no doubt as to the text's erotic import, brought home by Barnes's rhythmic use of present participles until the final cataclysmic or orgasmic crescendo when both human and beast collapse, laying down together in the final sentence of the text. As with Ackerley, the false question, the question that likewise tempts Barnes's critics, is whether we should read this, the book's closing scene, as a sexual encounter. The easy psychoanalytic answer, of course, is to construe the passage as a displaced scene of lesbian sexuality, with Nora's dog as the metaphor of his mistress. While such an interpretation lets us imagine a Barnes cleverly able to end her text with an act whose "realist" description could only have inflamed the potential charge of obscenity and risk of censorship, it also offers us, via the detour of metaphor, something that is nonetheless more comforting, less disturbing, and still less perverse than what the text presents on its literal level: that of a trans-species mating dance as unspeakable in its possible outcome as in its implications, which have been repeatedly foreshadowed in the text since Nora's first encounter with Robin at the circus. If the epitome of obscenity is reached in this scene of mock-aggressive, mock-erotic exchange where Robin mimes Nora's dog and starts "to bark also, crawling after him—barking in a fit of laughter, obscene and touching," is this because the beast is the hidden symbol of lesbian sexuality or because the essence of woman is recaptured in the beast? In Jane Marcus's words, "When the woman acts the beast and the beast turns human in the last scene, do we laugh or weep?"[14] Either possibility, revisionist or traditionally misogynist, presupposes an eminently *human* appreciation of what animality is, as if the nonhuman species exists in this view only as the repressed of the human species, which since Freud, we have understood to be sexuality itself. "Animals find their way about largely by the keenness of their nose," states at one point Doctor O'Connor in an apparent allusion to Freud's similar remarks in *Civilization and Its Discontents,* concluding likewise that "we have lost ours in order not to be one of them" (149). A humanism that would define humanity in antithesis to the beasts had better be careful not to exclude some vital part of human life, or it risks seeing the excluded, and therefore "animalistic," part return as the very truth of the human being.[15] The beast then becomes the key to understanding the (human) self. Far from being the radical other of a distinct species difference, the animal becomes but a degraded human. Where we expected to find something else, we find only ourselves. The beast becomes *stricto sensu* anthropomorphized,[16] in a way of seeing whose doleful consequences have long been visited not only on the world of animals but also on human beings of different races, genders, and classes: animals are reduced to being lesser humans, and subjected humans are treated as animals.

Another possible way to read the end of *Nightwood* is mythological rather than metaphorical, with Robin a lesbian counter-Actaeon to Nora's Diana/Madonna; here Diana's discovery of the intruder turns Actaeon not into a prey object but into another one of her hounds. Far from taking flight at the prospect of her beastly metamorphosis, Robin turns *toward* the dog in a paroxysm of play and aggression, cavorting with him, responding to his bark and bite with that "obscene and touching" bark of her own. To become one of Diana's minions, indifferently dog or nymph, is perhaps to recapture that "primitive innocence" Robin so desperately seeks. That innocence requires someone's permission, and Nora is to all intents and purposes the sole character capable of giving such a permission "to live." From Nora's point of view, of course, this is not a satisfactory closure, since there is no question of "possessing" Robin in either an erotic or a domestic sense. Present, she is only the legitimating observer; absent, the authorizing imago like the Madonna on the wall. What she does in either case is to allow her dependent creatures, female or beastly, to be themselves and not merely the negative poles of patriarchal repression. In this sense, she is truly affirmed as Diana, protectress of women and animals. What would then appear to be the book's ambiguous ending is really only the beginning of the Virgin deity's charge, which Nora assumes with full lucidity.[17]

CHAPTER 2

Colette at Home

If anyone has succeeded in carrying out, through her writing, the Dianic charge of protecting women and animals, not negatively, by vindicating and affirming a female power to inflict retribution, but positively, by celebrating domestic diversity, it would be Colette, a contemporary of both Wharton and Barnes. In Colette's case, the affirmation of that domesticity was also the birth of an author who turned the intimate and the quotidian into subject matter worthy of literature. The developing role of the beast in her work charts not only her trajectory as a writer but also her success in marking out a space all her own—a space, as we shall see, coterminous with the counter–public sphere we have labeled as that of Diana.

The beginnings of Colette's writing career, it is well known, are a far cry from such a utopian alternative, rooted as they are in her oppressive relation with the infamous Willy, described in her *Mes apprentissages* (1936) as an overbearing patriarch, an older man well established in Parisian society who married the young girl from the country, introduced her to the big city, then locked her in her room to write her schoolgirl memoirs, which would later be published under *his* name as *Claudine Goes to School* (1900) and would be followed by other "Claudine" novels all equally written by her but credited to him. Separated from Willy in 1904 and ultimately divorced in 1907, after her scandalously public affair with an aristocratic woman, the Marquise de Belbeuf, or "Missy," and an equally compromising stage and music-hall career, Colette eventually found her way as a writer by going back to her roots, to her mother and her mother's rustic menagerie of a home. Only then, after publishing *La maison de Claudine* (1922), translated into English as *My Mother's House,* could she emerge as the writer who signed her name simply "Colette."

For Colette became her pen name only by the slow process that defined her both as a writer and as a woman, and a woman who was indeed the daughter of her powerful mother, Sidonie or "Sido," whose name she shared. Born Sidonie Gabrielle Colette, Colette would first take the authorial name "Colette Willy," the result of joining her father's surname to her husband's pen name, itself a deformation of his patronymic, Gauthier-Villars. Signing her works with this name—ironically just as she began to separate from Willy—allowed her to recuperate and reclaim those works previously thought to have been written by Willy, as if to dislodge the priority of his name by preceding it with her father's own feminine-resonating patronymic. Interestingly, the first work signed by the name Colette Willy, the 1904 *Dialogues de bêtes (Creature Conversations),* sketches out the rural, animal-filled space that finds its full expression in the last work signed by that name, *My Mother's House.* These two works also chart that maternal domesticity whose problematic edges are then explored in later works, all of which are signed simply "Colette," a pen name that can be read as a woman's given name or as patriarchal surname. At the same time, "Colette" becomes the name of the author's literary persona in an increasingly baroque mix of narrative fiction and autobiographical reflections that has ensnared many an overly literal reader. Since my concern is less the "reality" of her references than the import of the domestic imaginary she presents in her work, the question of whether any particular use of the name "Colette" refers to the historical person of the writer or the fictional persona of a character is ultimately moot.

Dialogues de bêtes represents not only a first step toward authorship but also a radical change of genre from the salacious Claudine stories, from adolescent love novels to fictive animal conversations. In *Mes apprentissages,* Colette makes clear the connection between the change in writing and the changes in her domestic life:

> Je n'en étais pas encore à vouloir fuir le domicile conjugal, ni le travail plus conjugal que le domicile. Mais je changeais. Qu'importe que ce fût lentement! Le tout est de changer.
>
> Je m'éveillais vaguement à un devoir envers moi-même, celui d'écrire autre chose que les *Claudine.* Et, goutte à goutte, j'exsudais les *Dialogues*

de bêtes, où je me donnai le plaisir, non point vif, mais honorable, de ne pas parler de l'amour. . . . Je ne me suis reprise à mettre l'amour en romans, et à m'y plaire, que lorsque j'eus recouvré de l'estime pour lui—et pour moi.¹

[I had not yet reached the point of wishing to leave the "domestic hearth" or the work that was even more domestic than the hearth. But I was changing. Slowly, if you like, but what matter? To change is the great thing.

I had become vaguely aware of a duty toward myself, which was to write something other than the *Claudines.* And so, drop by drop, I sweated out the *Dialogues des bêtes.* In it I enjoyed the moderate but honorable satisfaction of not talking about love. . . . I brought love back into my books and found pleasure in it when I had recovered my esteem for it—and for myself.]²

Her "duty" to herself was to write something other than the kind of love stories written under Willy's tutelage and for his benefit. Not only the genre but the emotional category of love had been tainted by the arrangement with Willy and could again become a possible literary subject and imaginable affect only after Colette had "recovered esteem for it—and *for [herself].*" That this recovery process should take the form of a detour through the world of beasts expresses the central theme of this book and once again posits an alternative to the (masculinist) paradigm of the animal as mediator/obstacle to desire. For Colette, the animal world is the antidote to an exploitative patriarchal arrangement masquerading as love and marriage; a rapprochement with it requires strenuous labor ("que j'exsudais goutte à goutte") but is also the only chance for her ever to recover a concept of love worth wanting. The utopic alternative to her oppressive marriage had already taken clear shape in her mind as early as 1903, when she stated in an interview her dream to transform her house into a type of Noah's Ark ("faire de ma maison une Arche de Noé"): "Je n'ai qu'un rêve, vivre à la campagne, et là, dans la solitude de la montagne, réunir autour de moi tous les animaux domestiques possibles!" (I have but one dream, to live in the country, and there, in the mountain solitude, to bring together around me every possible domestic animal!)³ That dream was initially realized by her partial change of residence to Monts-Baucons, a small country property Willy owned outside Besançon, where he was only too glad to let her spend as much as five or six months out of the year, no doubt to pursue more readily his countless affairs in faraway Paris. Only with the official filing of divorce papers in 1907 was Colette forced to abandon a habitat she had come to cherish as a true home, a home whose loss she bemoaned ever after. For it was there, according to *Mes apprentissages,* that she had "faced the first hours of a new life, between my dog and my cat" [C'est là que j'ai affronté les premières heures d'une vie nouvelle, entre la chatte et le chien] (O, 3:1075/132–33).

First published in 1904 as a collection of four fictional conversations between her tiny bulldog, Toby-Chien, and her Chartreuse cat, Kiki-la-Doucette, the book was augmented and reissued in 1905 as *Sept dialogues de bêtes*, accompanied by a photographic reproduction of her portrait by the painter Jacques-Emile Blanche and an importantly legitimizing preface by the poet Francis Jammes. Later expanded and republished as *Douze dialogues de bêtes* in 1930, the collection spawned numerous other animal tales, typically published individually in Parisian journals before being themselves reissued in anthologies bearing titles like *Prrou, Poucette et quelques autres* (1913), *La paix chez les bêtes* (1916), *Paradis terrestres* (1932), *Chats* (1936), *De la patte à l'aile* (1943), and *Autres bêtes* (1949), or in some of Colette's other collected short texts: *Les vrilles de la vigne* (1908), *L'envers du music-hall* (1913), *Histoires pour Bel-Gazou* (1930), *L'étoile vesper* (1946), *Le fanal bleu* (1949).

A late symbolist poet known for his lyrical evocations of nature and "natural life" and at the time undergoing a reconversion to Catholicism, Francis Jammes was an ideal choice for "Colette Willy" to present herself as her own woman and to distance herself from her reputation as the disreputable young wife of a rather questionable Parisian writer and critic. Appearing as a true counterfather to the urbane, ambitious Willy, the austere and reclusive but kindly Jammes, though never having met Colette face to face, systematically rehabilitated her image, rejecting all rumors of her decadent Parisian life in favor of an idealized portrayal of her as the exemplary provincial homemaker:[4]

> Je dis donc que Mme Colette Willy n'eut jamais les cheveux courts; qu'elle ne s'habille point en homme; que son chat ne l'accompagne pas au concert; que la chienne de son amie ne boit pas que dans un verre à pied. Il est inexact que Mme Colette Willy travaille dans une cage à écureuil et qu'elle fasse du trapèze et des anneaux de telle sorte qu'elle touche, du pied, sa nuque.
> Mme Colette Willy n'a jamais cessé d'être la *femme bourgeoise* par excellence qui, levée à l'aube, donne de l'avoine au cheval, du maïs aux poules, des choux aux lapins, du séneçon au serin, des escargots aux canards, de l'eau de son aux porcs. A huit heures, été comme hiver, elle prépare le café au lait de sa bonne, et le sien. . . . Le rucher, le verger, le potager, l'étable, la basse-cour, la serre n'ont plus de secrets pour Mme Colette Willy.
> Mme Colette Willy n'est rien d'autre qui ne soit pas ce que je viens d'écrire. Je sais que, pour l'avoir rencontrée dans le monde, certains s'obstinèrent à la

compliquer. . . . Mme Colette Willy est une femme vivante, une femme *pour tout de bon,* qui a osé être naturelle et qui ressemble beaucoup plus à une petite mariée villageoise qu'à une littératrice perverse. (O, 2:4–5)

[I shall say, therefore, that Mme. Colette Willy never wore her hair cut short, that she does not dress up as a man, that her cat does not go to the concert with her, that her girlfriend's bitch does not drink out of a wine glass. It is not correct that Mme. Colette Willy works out in a squirrel cage and that while on the trapeze or the rings she manages to touch the back of her neck with her feet.

Mme. Colette Willy has never ceased to be the *bourgeois wife par excellence* who is up with the dawn, gives oats to the horse, corn to the hens, cabbage to the rabbits, groundsel to the canaries, snails to the ducks, and bran-water to the hogs. At eight o'clock, whether summer or winter, she makes café au lait for her maid, and for herself. . . . The beehive, the orchard, the vegetable garden, the stable, the poultry yard have no secrets left for Mme. Colette Willy.

Mme. Colette Willy is not otherwise than what I have just written. I know that, because of having met her in society, some individuals insist on making her complicated. . . . Mme. Colette Willy is a living woman, a woman *once and for all,* who has dared to be natural and who resembles a little village wife much more than a perverse woman of letters.]

Were it not for the actual changes going on in Colette's life and work, one would be inclined to see Jammes as either intentionally or unintentionally playing into a cynical public relations stunt on the part of the aspiring writer, exactly the kind of behavior for which Willy was famous. And while Jammes's portrayal of her as "une petite mariée villageoise" may border on the ridiculous, and his steadfast denial of the eccentricities of the Parisian legend that were indeed facts (her short hair, occasional cross-dressing, acrobatic workouts, etc.) may seem deluded, he does in fact have a correct inkling of Colette's true scandalousness in her "daring to be natural." The unfathomableness of the scandal, at least for the Catholic Jammes, and no doubt also for the self-absorbed Willy, was that the little village girl and the perverse writer were one and the same. Jammes glimpsed the woman writer's *daring* to reveal herself as she believed herself to be, not as her husband and the fashionable French socialites of the day believed her to be on the basis of the *Claudine* stories, or even as the pastorally inclined Jammes believed her to be. This powerful autobiographical impulse, of course, would generate Colette's voluminous opus as she strenuously sought from one work to the next to define herself beyond the imaginary categories of patriarchal condescension—neither as *ingénue* nor as *libertine* but as *ingénue libertine* both at once, to gloss the title of the last book published by "Colette Willy" before her divorce from Willy was finalized in 1910.

Sept dialogues de bêtes offers, in addition to Jammes's rehabilitory preface, a visual image of Colette in Jacques-Emile Blanche's 1905 portrait, which appears facing the title page.[5] Here we see sitting on a bed against a dark background an indeed short-haired Colette who is nonetheless wearing a frilly evening dress that reveals much of her neck, shoulder, and upper chest. The image manages to be at once modest and suggestive—truly "ingénue libertine." Innocently garbed in white and caught in a pose of reverie, the subject also exposes herself in an alluring way to the gaze, offering her bared neck for a possible caress. Yet the ostensibly male gaze that erotically organizes the field of perspective is broken by another gaze that emanates from the right foreground, where a tiny brindle bulldog (Toby-Chien) looks up directly into his mistress's eyes. To the lower right, an almost indiscernible cat (Kiki-la-Doucette) sits upright deep in the shadows, forward and slightly downward. The image is highly reminiscent of Titian's famous painting of a courtesan with her little dog, but in a turn-of-the-century bourgeois mode. Toby-Chien's watchful eye, as he sits partially enveloped by the folds of his mistress's dress and under the protection of her outstretched left arm, bespeaks an intimacy that outrivals the voyeurism of any spectator—an intimacy not entangled in false contradictions between virginity and lubricity but instead clearly assertive of a communal and affective bond beyond words.

Jammes grasps at this hint of something beyond the conventions of dutiful country wife and urban sophisticate when, in the middle of ebulliently extolling her appearance on the literary scene as "la poétesse" who will cast down all the other "muses fardées, laurées, cothurnées et lyrées" from Mount Parnassus, he remarks upon her presenting "son bull bringé et son chat avec autant d'assurance que Diane son lévrier ou qu'une Bacchante son tigre" [her brindle bulldog and her cat with as much self-assurance as Diana her greyhound or a Bacchante her tiger] (*O*, 2:5). Jammes conjures up the conflicted erotic thrill/terror of these images of an alliance between women and animals that leaves man their common object of prey, and while Toby-Chien and Kiki-la-Doucette may appear comfortably small and tame compared to their grander, fiercer relations, they do draw on the same traditions and affects. What is here foregrounded by the comparison is the woman author's "assurance" or self-confidence in presenting the first literary production to appear in her name, an assurance—whether naive or brazen, it is not clear—worthy of a virgin goddess who keeps the company of beasts. Or is it her being surrounded by beasts, canine and feline, that gives her the assurance that comes from a certain self-sufficiency, from needing no one, particularly no patriarchal figure, and from being ensconced in a domestic space she herself has defined and chosen?

The literary work being presented with such assurance as the first work of "Colette Willy" features the imaginary conversations of her pets, whose names she has not even bothered to change. While not wholly unprecedented, the *Dialogues de bêtes* was received as if it marked the invention of a whole new genre of literature (just as earlier the *Claudine* novels were seen to have launched an entirely new *type* of character).[6] And, indeed, in a way that despite the surface similarity has nothing to do with literary modernism per se, Colette's work is punctuated by a remarkable series of unprecedentedly new types of writing, all developed in the course of her passionately sustained effort to understand, define, and reveal her self. From *Claudine à l'école* (1900) to *La fanal bleu* (*The Blue Lantern*, 1949), whether she is writing schoolgirl memoirs, dialogues between animals, free recollections of her mother and the ambiance of the maternal home, novels of consummate lyricism that unflinchingly dissect the vicissitudes of intimacy, or vignettes of daily life, Colette manages to legitimate and elevate genres of writing that before her were not given serious credence as literature. To be precise, her writing is less the experimental creation of new forms à la high modernism than the literary affirmation and exploration of the polymorphously domestic spaces inhabited not by the heroism of great men and great deeds but by the everyday tragedy and comedy of women, children, and animals.

Such is the world we see in the animal dialogues, where Toby-Chien and Kiki-la-Doucette react to what from their point of view are major events: a storm, a train ride, an unexpectedly late dinner, the illness of their mistress (Elle), the ill temper of their master (Lui). Although *Lui* and *Elle* are described ironically as "seigneurs de moindre importance" (lords of lesser importance), the pathos (and humor!) of the dialogues comes from the utter dependency of the two animals upon their humans, to whom they refer with mock disdain as the "Deux Pattes" (Two-Paws). Both cat and dog are fully developed characters with distinctive personalities: Toby is anxious, emotional, overactive, eager to please those lesser important lords, He and She, but somehow always ending up in trouble with them; Kiki is diffident, cerebral, manipulative, and disdainful of everyone and manages to get away with most everything, typically getting Toby to take the fall for him. Their interaction provides a comedy of opposites as they react in differing ways to the all-but-incomprehensible behavior of the humans who lord over the house, such as telling Toby and Kiki to "shush" when, as they remark, they haven't made a peep and the human footsteps are so loud they would awaken a "deaf mouse." The result is a charming and satirical reversal of perspective on a typical bourgeois household, seen from the vantage point of those who have the least say in how things are done but are the most affected by those decisions. "He" mysteriously wastes all his time "scratching" paper next to a foul-smelling bottle of bluish-black liquid, which the animals can only assume is something he drinks. "She" gets so lost in her gardening she forgets to prepare dinner till late and is characterized by an unpredictable mix of smothering affection and ill-tempered rejection. A lick of her hand may garner either a slap on the snout or an embrace so tight as to make breathing impossible. Still, and in a fashion that already prefigures the much more elaborate domestic utopias we will encounter later, a certain nostalgia creeps in with the satisfaction of basic needs in this multispecies home: good food, a warm place by the fire, affection from others.

The affective universe of the household peopled with animals is significantly amplified in *Les vrilles de la vigne* (*The Tendrils of the Vine;* 1908), a set of short sketches, dialogues, and stories. The first of these, bearing the same name as the collection as a whole, spins an elaborate metaphor linking the mythic origin of the nightingale's nocturnal chant to the author's discovery of her own voice. Briefly, the nightingale was originally a day bird, sleeping soundly and quietly all through the night, until one evening it took its sleep in a vine, whose shoots grew so thickly and quickly that the poor bird found itself dangerously entangled and bound by them when it awoke the following morning. Having succeeded in struggling itself free, the nightingale decided henceforth to sing all night to keep itself from falling asleep in the treacherous vine, whence the origin of its time-honored nocturnal chant. Colette presents herself in analogy with the nightingale, having broken free from the clutches of her own domestic vine (her marriage to Willy) and in so doing discovered her own voice as a writer: "Quand la torpeur d'une nouvelle nuit de miel a pesé sur mes paupières, j'ai craint les vrilles de la vigne et j'ai jeté tout haut une plainte qui m'a revelé ma voix!" (When the torpor of a new honeymoon weighed on my eyelids, I feared the tendrils of the vine and I uttered a loud lament that revealed my voice to me).⁷ Colette apparently attached such importance to this text that she revised it continually from edition to edition even as late as its inclusion in her 1949 *Oeuvres complètes*.⁸ Even the odious Willy had his chance to comment, being (as he still was at the time of first publication) her legal husband and literary editor: "Continuez donc, petite horreur charmante!" (Keep on going, you charming little horror), he wrote in the margins (*O*, 1:1531).

The myth of the nightingale is, of course, Colette's own story told at a moment when she had not yet fully broken free of Willy and found the right direction in which to fly. This was a period of great personal experimentation in Colette's life, from her lesbian relations (with Missy, among others) to her acting career (including stage appearances in the nude or as a cat), to music-hall tours and idyllic interludes in the countryside at Monts-Baucons. All of these become the subject matter of chapters in *Les vrilles de la vigne*, which are as diverse in style and genre as in content, from more animal dialogues ("Toby-Chien parle," "Dialogue de bêtes"—both of these later inserted into reprints of the *Dialogues de bêtes*) to veritable prose poems, erotic fantasies, dream scenarios, satirical tales, a kind of vacation journal, and recollections of life in music shows. For Colette as for the nightingale, the important thing was not to get lulled back into a restrictive domestic arrangement. Interestingly, the patriarchal enclosure is described by a metaphor from nature (the vine) rather than the more predictably cultural one of the cage, gilded or not. The danger of entrapment is one the bird encounters from being out in the wild, as opposed to the kind of cozy, comfortable home life enjoyed, despite their complaints and anxieties, by Toby and Kiki. Or, more precisely, it is the very coziness and comfort of that home life that lulls one into not noticing the slowly strangulating grip of the vine as it grows ever so surreptitiously.

The struggle to break free from those creeping bonds is witnessed in the dialogue "Toby-Chien parle" by none other than the intrepid little "bull" himself, who quivers under the carpet while "Elle" explodes in rage at her absent spouse. "He" is, of course, out on the town with three or four of his "tortoises" hanging onto him, each one outdoing the other to claim herself as "the true Claudine" (*O*, 1:995). The "tortoises" are, of course, His mistresses, but Toby has misunderstood, hearing the word *tortues* for *tourterelles* (literally turtledoves but figuratively lovebirds). Transferentially yelling at the frightened, perplexed Toby in the place of the absent husband ("Tu m'entends, crapaud bringé, excessif petit bull cardiaque!" (D'you understand me, you brindled toad, you heart-case of a little bull-dog!),[9] Elle finally bursts out with a long list of personal desires, which unsurprisingly reproduce the same spectrum of rebellious acts committed by Colette herself as part and parcel of her long, drawn-out process of disentangling herself from Willy's web:

> Je veux faire ce que je veux. Je veux jouer la pantomime, même la comédie. Je veux danser nue, si le maillot me gêne et humilie ma plastique. Je veux me retirer dans une île, s'il me plaît, ou fréquenter des dames qui vivent de leurs charmes, pourvu qu'elles soient gaies, fantasque, voire mélancoliques et sages, comme sont beaucoup de femmes de joie. Je veux écrire des livres tristes et chastes, où il n'y aura que des paysages, des fleurs, du chagrin, de la fierté, et la candeur des animaux charmants qui s'effraient de l'homme. (O, 1:994)
>
> [I want to do as I please. I want to play in pantomime and even in comedy. If I find tights uncomfortable and degrading to my body, I want to dance naked. I want to retire to an island if I feel like it, or consort with ladies who live by their charms, as long as they're gay and amusing, or even melancholy and wise as so many ladies of easy virtue are. I want to write sad, pure books about nothing but flowers and landscapes, sorrow and pride, and the innocence of charming animals who fear mankind.] (125)

Doing what one wants means acting, dancing in the nude, retiring to an island, frequenting women of ill repute, and writing books, especially books featuring landscapes, flowers, and animals. Why should writing about animals appear in Colette's imaginary on a par with the most daring acts of personal and sexual liberation? Why not, given the way she seized her authorial identity by leaving the topic of love for that of talking pets? Given the inspirational metaphor of the nightingale finding the beauty of its voice when it first sings out of fear of falling asleep amid the treacherous vines of patriarchally organized family life? Given the fear and distrust of men that she shares with the animals? And given the manifestly transferential role of the beast in allowing the character of Elle to vent the desires smothered by an all-too-traditional bourgeois marriage, and in so venting to allow the author, Colette, to defend her own very public and scandalous change of lifestyle (despite Jammes's well-intentioned words)? Elle's outburst achieves its paroxysm when, interrupted by Toby's upset panting, she takes notice of him and then, in an act analogous to that of Robin Vote, gets down on all fours in imitation of a dog:

> TOBY-CHIEN: . . . Je haletais autant qu'Elle, ému de sa violence. Elle entendit ma respiration et se jeta à quatre pattes, sa tête sous le tapis de la table, contre la mienne . . .

Je voyais la brume de ses cheveux danser autour de sa tête qu'"Elle hochait furieusement. Elle était comme moi à quatre pattes, aplatie, comme un chien qui va s'élancer, et j'espérais un peu qu'Elle aboierait . . .

KIKI-LA-DOUCETTE, *révolté:* Aboyer, Elle! Elle a ses défauts, mais tout de même, aboyer! . . . Si Elle devait parler en quatre-pattes, elle miaulerait.

TOBY-CHIEN, *poursuivant:* Elle n'aboya point, en effet. Elle se redressa d'un bond, rejeta en arrière les cheveux qui lui balayaient le visage . . . (*O,* 1:996)

[TOBY-DOG: . . . I was so affected by her violence that by then I was panting as hard as She was. She heard me and went down on all fours, with her head close to mine under the table-cover . . .

She shook her head so violently that I saw the cloud of her hair dance all around it. She was on all fours like me, flattened like a dog about to spring, and I couldn't help hoping She'd bark.

KIKI-THE-DEMURE (*shocked*): She, bark! She has her faults, but all the same, barking! If She had to speak like a four-footed one, She'd mew.

TOBY-DOG (*continuing*): Anyhow, She didn't bark. She sprang to her feet, tossed back the hair that was brushing her face . . .] (127–28)

Framed by Kiki's comic rejoinder, asserting the superiority of cats over dogs, the passage pinpoints the moment when Elle rediscovers and reaffirms a powerful new sense of self in the act of becoming the beast. Colette deftly avoids here the ideological trap that ensnares Djuna Barnes when she equates the feminine and the animal in the desire to vindicate the rights of women to a social and sexual self-definition. In Colette's case, what matters is not to have become the beast in some way but to have identified with the beast to the point of recognizing one's similarity to and *difference* from the beast as the key to an affirmation of one's gendered self. Elle, unlike Robin, precisely stops short of barking like the dog, stands back up, and renews her diatribe with ever greater eloquence when she vows no longer to attend boring social events, like tea parties and exhibition openings, and no longer to be a spectator at theatrical premieres but instead to embrace the protean figure of the actress:

> Je n'irai plus aux premières—sinon de l'autre côté de la rampe. Car je danserai encore sur la scène, je danserai nue ou habillée, pour le seul plaisir de danser, d'accorder mes gestes au rythme de la musique, de virer, brûlée de lumière, aveuglée comme une mouche dans un rayon . . . Je danserai, j'inventerai de belles danses lentes où le voile parfoir me couvrira, parfois m'environna comme une spirale de fumée, parfois se tendra derrière ma course comme la toile d'une barque . . . Je serai la statue, le vase animé, la bête bondissante, l'arbre balancé, l'esclave ivre . . . (*O,* 1:997)

[I'll never go to a premiere again, except on the other side of the footlights. Because I mean to go on dancing on stage, and I shall dance naked or clothed for the sheer pleasure of dancing, of suiting my gestures to the rhythm of the music and spinning round ablaze with light, blind as a fly in a sunbeam ... And I shall invent beautiful slow dances with a veil; sometimes it will cover my body, sometimes it will envelop me with a spiral of smoke, and when I run it will billow behind me like the sail of a ship. I shall be a statue, a vase that comes to life, a leaping animal, a tree swaying in the wind, a drunken slave ...] (129)

But as she goes on to caution Toby-Chien again, now recognizing him to be the dog that he is and not the transferential surrogate, to become all these things is absolutely *not* to give in to some urge for self-abnegation or abjection but rather to acquire nothing less than a sense of dignity and self-worth: "Qui donc a osé murmurer, trop près de mon oreille irritable, les mots de décheance, d'avilissement? ... Toby-Chien, Chien de bon sens, écoute bien: je ne me suis jamais sentie plus digne de moi-même!" [Who then has dared to whisper, too close to my irritable ear, the words of decline, of debasement? ... Toby-Dog, Dog of good sense, listen carefully: never have I felt more worthy of myself!] (*O*, 1:997/129, trans. modified).

This remarkable text is not just, however, a polemical vindication on Colette's part of her newfound freedoms in breaking from Willy but a profound statement, early on in her opus, of Colette's ethic of love, adventure, zest for life, and constant awareness of the joys and risks of alterity. Love, "she" tells Toby-Chien, is a conscious beautifying or "embellishing" of the other whereby one both draws strength and vulnerability: "Non, Toby-Chien. Moi, j'aime! J'aime tant tout ce que j'aime! Si tu savais comme j'embellis tout ce que j'aime, et quel plaisir je me donne en aimant! Si tu pouvais comprendre de quelle force et de quelle défaillance m'emplit ce que j'aime!" [No, Toby-Dog, I do love. And when I love anything I love it utterly. If you knew how I embellish everything I love, and all the pleasure I get out of loving! If you could understand the wonderful mix of strength and weakness with which the things I love fill me!] (*O*, 1:996/127). Such a love, "she" goes on to say, is to be grazed or caressed by happiness itself, a kind of epiphany she describes in starkly beautiful language that poetically condenses the sexual and the animal with the nostalgic ambiance of the countryside:

C'est cela que je nomme le frôlement du bonheur ... caresse impalpable qui creuse le long de mon dos un sillon velouté, comme le bout d'une aile creuse l'onde ... Frisson mystérieux prêt à se fondre en larmes, angoisse légère que je cherche et qui m'atteint devant un cher paysage argenté de brouillard, devant un ciel où fleurit l'aube, sous le bois où l'automne souffle une haleine mûre et musquée . . . Tristesse voluptueuse des fins de jour, bondissement sans cause d'un coeur plus mobile que celui du chevreuil, tu es le frôlement même du bonheur, toi qui gis au sein des heures les plus pleines . . . et jusqu'au fond du regard de ma sûre amie . . . (*O*, 1:996)

[It's that that I call the caress of happiness. The caress of happiness . . . an impalpable touch that traces a velvety furrow all down my back, as a wing tip furrows a wave . . . A strange quivering on the brink of tears, that slight, expected anguish which seizes me before a dear landscape silvered with mist, or a sky where dawn is breaking, or in woods where the breath of autumn is honeyed and mellow . . . The voluptuous sadness of the day's end, the upleaping for no reason of a heart more restless than a deer's—you are the authentic caress of happiness, which lies hidden in the heart of the richest hours . . . and in the depths of the eyes of she who is my sure friend . . .] (127)

The happiness of love in all its risk and its ambiguity caresses her as one would affectionately stroke a favorite pet's back, parting its fur, or as a wingtip skims a wave. The caress of happiness is paradoxically described as a "strange quivering on the brink of tears" or a "slight anguish" both sought and found in the wooded landscape we will only later understand to be rooted in the childhood memory of the maternal home in the country, a nostalgic homeland that Colette, at the time she wrote this, was beginning to rediscover while spending much time at Monts-Baucons. The happiness and love re-evoked by that landscape is always a kind of liminal experience, the rediscovery of herself in the encounter with alterity, an experience thus associated with the change of light associated with daybreak or twilight, or the change of seasons signaled by the autumn breeze. The caress of happiness is simultaneously a "voluptuous sadness," a paradoxical blend of joy and gloom, an intense restlessness of the heart comparable only to that of a deer and found in the evening glow or in the eyes of a lover (clearly marked as feminine here: "ma sûre amie"). And so it is that the dignity of love itself is recaptured as the writer's own sense of dignity is reclaimed, by the dialogical encounter with other beings where the closeness of contact is also the affectionate acknowledgment of difference, where the purity, the intensity of love is found in a close approach to the other that stops just short of becoming the other. Such is the lesson of these "dialogues between beasts."

The lesson of love achieves the analytical perfection of a fable in another chapter of *Les vrilles de la vigne*, "Nonoche," the story of a mother cat drawn by the call of a distant tomcat, all the more in that she is lucidly aware of absolutely everything that call implies, its promise of pleasure and menace of pain. Nonoche is also the first mother figure to appear overtly in Colette's opus, the mother so conspicuously absent, for example, from the *Claudine* novels. And it is as a mother that we first see this tricolored cat (orange, black, and white) after an opening description that sets us in the beautiful countryside of the Monts-Baucons. The time, unsurprisingly given our earlier discussions, is sunset, and Nonoche contemplates the beauty of her latest kitten, her young son still sleeping curled up against her in their basket. Nonoche is depicted as an archetypal female, young and beautiful even though already many times a mother: "En dépit de nombreuses maternités, Nonoche conserve un air enfantin qui trompe sur son âge. Sa beauté solide restera longtemps jeune, et rien dans sa démarche, dans sa taille svelte et plate, ne révèle qu'elle fut, en quatre portées, dix-huit fois mère." (Despite her many pregnancies, Nonoche maintains a childish air which makes her look young for her age. Her solid beauty will long remain young, for nothing in her gait, in her slender and flattened figure, gives it away that she has been, through four litters, eighteen times a mother.)[10] As the twilight turns to dusk, her taking pride in the beauty of her creation leads to her recognition that there remains only one thing to be done for him, namely to wean him: "Je ne vois plus rien à faire pour lui, sauf de le sevrer" (O, 1:989). At the same time that Nonoche comes to grips with the final gesture in fulfillment of her maternal duty, she also becomes prey to vague, empty feelings of longing and melancholia: "Un miaulement de convoitise et de désoeuvrement lui échappe. Elle s'ennuie. Depuis quelque temps, chaque crépuscule ramène cette mélancholie agacée, ce vide et vague désir" [A mewing of lust and indolence escapes her. She is bored. For some time now, every dusk brings back this irritable melancholia, this empty and vague longing] (O, 1:990).

In this frame of mind Nonoche becomes susceptible to the tom's mournful cry from deep in the woods where it is already night, a cry whose melancholy echoes her own feelings of loss:

> Du fond du bois où la nuit massive est descendue d'un bloc, par-dessus l'or immobile des treilles, à travers tous les bruits familiers, n'a-t-elle pas entendu venir jusqu'à elle, trainant, sauvage, musical, insidieux—l'Appel du Matou?
>
> Elle écoute . . . Plus rien. Elle s'est trompée . . . Non! L'appel retentit de nouveau, lointain, rauque et mélancolique à faire pleurer, reconnaissable entre tous. (O, 1:991)

[From the depths of the woods where night has fallen, immense, all at once, over the still gold of the trellises, beyond all the familiar sounds, did she not hear something languid, wild, musical, and insidious beckon towards her—the Call of the Tomcat?

She listens . . . Nothing more. She was wrong . . . No! The call rings out again, distant, hoarse and melancholic enough to make one cry, unmistakable from all others.]

Lost in the shadows, his voice bespeaks the very darkness of desire: "Sa voix s'exhale du bois noir, comme la voix même de l'ombre" [His voice exhales from the black woods, like the very voice of the shadows] (O, 1:991). The dark awakening of desire, the voice that calls out in the night, all this has nothing to do with any romantic conception of beauty or love. The force of eros is overpowering, sublime, and this text wondrously does nothing to mitigate—indeed, it all too lucidly amplifies—that force, attractive and terrifying all at once, attractive in and despite its very terror. The tom freely describes himself in less than attractive terms:

> Tu ne connais pas mon visage et qu'importe! Avec orgueil, je t'apprends qui je suis: je suis le long Matou déguenillé par dix étés, durci par dix hivers. Une des mes pattes boite en souvenir d'une vieille blessure, mes narines balafrées grimacent et je n'ai plus qu'une oreille, festonné par la dent de mes rivaux.
>
> A force de coucher par terre, la terre m'a donné sa couleur. . . . Mes flancs vides se touchent et ma peau glisse autour des mes muscles secs, entraînés au rapt et au viol . . . Et toute cette laideur me fait pareil à l'Amour! Viens! . . . Quand je paraîtrai à tes yeux, tu ne reconnaîtras rien de moi—que l'Amour!" (O, 1:991)

[You don't know my face, but what does it matter! With pride, I will teach you who I am: I am the long Tomcat, run ragged from ten summers, hardened by ten winters. I limp on one of my paws out of remembrance for an old wound, my scarred nostrils make a strange face and I have only one ear left, festooned by the teeth of my rivals.

By dint of sleeping on the ground, the earth has given me its color. . . . My cavernous flanks touch each other and my skin slides over my taut muscles, well skilled in abduction and rape . . . And all of this ugliness makes me similar to Love! Come! . . . When I appear before your eyes, you will recognize nothing of me—only Love!]

In sum, his very hideousness makes him irresistible; despite his decrepitude he is seductive *because* he incarnates passionate love itself. Unlike human seducers, however, the tom is no deceiver and tells Nonoche in brutally frank and lucidly unglamorous terms exactly what will happen between them: "Mes dents courberont ta nuque rétive, je souillerai ta robe, je t'infligerai autant de morsures que de caresses, j'abolirai en toi le souvenir de ta demeure et tu seras, pendant des jours et des nuits, ma sauvage compagne hurlante" [My teeth will curve your recalcitrant nape, I will soil your dress, I will inflict as many bites as kisses on you, I will make you forget all about your home and, for days and nights, you will be my wild, howling companion] (O, 1:991–92). The violence and intense savagery of this passion will be followed, continues the tom, by the ever deepening darkness of her abandonment by him and her weary return home, where, exhausted, she will nonetheless keep alive their love in her dreams—and, no doubt, in her womb, where a new life will commence:

> jusqu'à l'heure plus noire où tu te retrouveras seule, car j'aurai fui, mystérieusement, las de toi, appelé par celle que je ne connais pas, celle que je n'ai pas possédée encore . . . Alors tu retourneras vers ton gîte, affamée, humble, vêtue de boue, les yeux pâles, l'échine creusée comme si ton fruit y pesait déjà, et tu te réfugieras dans un long sommeil tressaillant de rêves où ressuscitera notre amour . . . Viens! (O, 1:992)
>
> [until that even darker hour when you will find yourself all alone, for I will have mysteriously fled, weary of you, called by she whom I do not know, she whom I have not yet possessed . . . Then, will you return to your place of abode, hungry, humble, cloaked in mud, pale-eyed, your back broken as if already weighed down by your fruit, and you will take refuge in a long slumber shuddering with dreams in which you will resuscitate our love . . . Come!]

Nothing the tom tells Nonoche, of course, is news to her, since she has already been through this before. She listens, careful not to let on that she is caught in an internal struggle between the desire to answer's the tom's call and the desire to resist its temptation: "Nonoche écoute. Rien dans son attitude ne décèle qu'elle lutte contre elle-même, car le tentateur pourrait la voir à travers l'ombre, et le mensonge est la première parure d'une amoureuse . . . Elle écoute, rien de plus . . ." [Nonoche listens. Nothing in her attitude reveals that she is struggling with herself, for the tempter might be able to see her though the shadows, and lying is the first display of a woman in love . . . She listens, nothing more] (O, 1:992). The tom is what in our contemporary parlance we would call "rough trade," yet this remarkable text of Colette unflinchingly understands *both* the danger of such sexual encounters *and* their thrill.

Pondering what to do, Nonoche is distracted by her son, who is now fully awake and who wants to engage his mother is some playful kitten antics. He pounces on her only to be rudely beaten back, "so surprised he doesn't dare ask why, or dare to follow she who will never again be his nurse and who goes off head held high, down the black little alleyway and out toward the haunted woods . . ." [si étonné qu'il n'ose pas demander pourquoi, ni suivre celle qui ne sera plus jamais sa nourrice et qui s'en va très digne, le long de la petite allée noire, vers le bois hanté . . .] (O, 1:992).

This beautiful text, ironically dedicated to "Willy" of all people, is doubly scandalous to patriarchal values, a true feminist fable. For maternity here is fulfilled, not by infinitely giving oneself to one's child, but by bringing "him" to the point where separation is not only good but necessary for both mother and child, and love is the fleeting embrace of violent passion with the most disreputable of partners. On the one hand, "Nonoche" shows that the mother and not the father lays down the law of castration, the infamous *nom* or *non du père* of psychoanalysis, which Freudian science has misrecognized in the place of *the non de la mère*. On the other hand, female sexual desire is positively represented in Nonoche's response—dark though it may be—to the echo of its need in the tom's mating call, whose own "melancholy" mirrors that of the mother ready to wean her child. That desire is fulfilled in the rough-and-tumble of the passionate embrace, the temporary release from all decorum, with no romantic expectation—or even projection—of any permanent arrangement with the chosen partner. Marriage is not the gilded horizon of love in this story, and Nonoche runs the risk/pleasure of sexual adventure to come home bearing her next child. "Nonoche" thus reinforces the lesson of the nightingale in "The Tendrils of the Vine," although now the negative threat of entrapment by romantic/patriarchal bonds is presented as the positive freedom of the mother cat, who asserts her liberty of desire and her independence from both kitten and tom, both sons and lovers. Under the cover, then, of this cat fable, patriarchy is dealt a double blow while a true matriarchal imaginary is set in place.

The stage is now set for Colette's rediscovery of the domestic bliss associated with her mother's house as a utopic counterdomestic space. Hints of that nostalgized space of the maternal abode inhabited by animals and surrounded by woods are present in her previous works: the *Claudine* novels themselves hearken back to the happy childhood spent in provincial Puisaye, and as early as the first *Claudine* novel the heroine maintains a special bond with her cat, Fanchette. Other pets, including Toby-Chien himself under his own name, are introduced in subsequent installments of the series. In addition to the appearance in the novels of her pets as characters, there is the social zoology of her human characters, richly developed by means of animal metaphors: the lecherous Dutertre is wolflike, various schoolgirl friends bear differing feline characteristics, the lesbian schoolteachers are dovelike, Armand the music instructor is like a wild bird, and so on. Finally, while *Colette à l'école* is ostensibly set in the Puisaye region, with repeated lyrical evocations of the woods and meadows already in a style worthy of the mature Colette, the parental home is crucially different from Colette's childhood abode in at least one respect: the total absence of the mother. This absence is all the more surprising given Colette's deep attachment to her mother, frequent letter writing to her even during the "Willy" years, and later deep commitment to her mother's memory through her writing of at least three entire books and numerous short pieces in which "Sido" emerges as a pivotal character. There is a father figure in Claudine's home, to be sure, but he is an absent presence in a thoroughly conventional way, a doddering *papa* more engrossed in his ongoing research on the region's slug varieties (to be published as his pretentiously titled *Malacologie du Fresnois*) than concerned with the doings of his own daughter, even though he supposedly "tient lieu de maman" [holds the mother's place] (O, 1:13). This repression of the maternal, even from *within* the fictional world narrated by Colette, is no doubt the most poignant testimonial to the utter domination and destitution of her being by the relentlessly patriarchal Willy.

So once again to correct the glaring absence of the mother and once again to free herself from the patriarchal imaginary, she daringly gives to the book known in English translation as *My Mother's House* the title *La maison de Claudine (Claudine's House)*. To restore the figure of the mother to the fictional world of Claudine is, for Colette, to restore that world to herself as well, to reclaim what is most hers in the Claudine stories and to reclaim through her writing a lost ambiance.[11] *My Mother's House* is a series of sketches and reminiscences that begin with an evocation of Sido calling from her porch for her children, hidden away in the foliage like cats and, like cats, coming home only when it suits them. After about two dozen such vignettes describing her mother and the family's home life, the final nine chapters present Colette herself as a maternal figure, busy with her daughter and a bevy of different animals. Reclaiming the mother for "Claudine" leads Colette to reclaim motherhood for herself and to present herself as a matriarch every bit as wise and self-possessed as Sido. And just as Sido named "Colette" Sidonie after herself but called her familiarly by the affectionate nickname "Minet-Chéri," so Colette would bestow upon her daughter her own given name of Colette but also the affectionate nickname "Bel-Gazou."

If any section in this book gives us a sense of the atmosphere of in Sido's household, it is the chapter headed "My Mother and the Animals." The tenth chapter in the order of the book's presentation, its pivotal role is revealed by the chronological order in which the chapters were initially written and published as individual pieces in journals. "My Mother and the Animals" was the sixth piece in the order of composition but the first to mark the mother as the book's central character, as indicated by the title.[12] More to the point, the text not only situates the mother within the household full of various creatures but also presents her as the principle that binds together that polyvalent domesticity.

As if to mimic Colette's own slow return to and rediscovery of the maternal home in all its creaturely plenitude, the chapter begins by detailing Colette's earliest memories, not of La Puisaye, but of Paris. These are enumerated according to her three successive trips there, between ages six and thirteen, all evidently unpleasant and the last of which left her with a distinctly negative impression, namely "the surprise and the melancholy aversion aroused in me by what I called houses without animals" [l'étonnement, l'aversion mélancolique de ce que je nommais les maisons sans bêtes] (O, 1:998/48). The home without animals is readily assimilated to a space without life:

> Ces cubes sans jardins, ces logis sans fleurs où nul chat ne miaule derrière la porte de la salle à manger, où l'on n'écrase pas, devant la cheminée, un coin du chien traînant comme un tapis, ces appartements privés d'esprits familiers, où la main, en quête de cordiale caresse, se heurte au marbre, au bois, au velours inanimés. (O, 1:999)

> [Mere cubes without gardens, flowerless abodes where no cat mews behind the dining-room door, where one never treads near the fireside on some part of a dog sprawling like a rug; rooms devoid of familiar spirits, wherein the hand seeking a friendly caress encounters only inanimate wood, or marble, or velvet.] (48)

In contrast, upon returning to the maternal home, the narrator discovers the integral unity of a domestic space composed of diverse living beings: "Comme si je les découvrais ensemble, je saluai, inséparables, ma mère, le jardin et la ronde des bêtes" [As if I were discovering them all together again, I extended my composite greeting to my mother, the garden, and the circle of animals] (*O*, 1:999/48–49). This diversity of life grasped simultaneously in its multiplicity is a key theme of the maternal home as represented by Colette. Not just a single pet, or even a single species, but an entire menagerie, a virtual "Noah's ark," makes for the magic of Sido's *ménage*: "Que tout était féerique et simple, parmi cette faune de la maison natale" [All was faery and yet simple among the fauna of my early home] (*O*, 1:1000/51).

The first example of this "Sidonian" fauna to appear to the narrator's eyes is none other than Nonoche, the mother cat, who has just given birth to a litter of kittens, followed by another litter birthed by Nonoche's daughter, Bijou, while the Havanese bitch, Musette, "intarissable en bâtards" [perennial breeder of bastards] (*O*, 1:999/49), takes care of her latest pup. The cat basket is now "overflowing with indistinguishable cats" [débordante de chats indistincts], described as so "many treasures [that] had bloomed in [the narrator's] absence!" [Que de trésors éclos en mon absence!] (*O*, 1:999/49). In the midst of this proliferating mass of feline paws and mouths is found the peculiar sight of Bijou sucking on one of Nonoche's teats while nursing her own newborns below. Nothing that should leave us overastonished, we are told:

> Je n'étais pas surprise de cette chaîne de chattes s'allaitant l'une à l'autre. A qui vit aux champs et se sert de ses yeux, tout devient miraculeux et simple. Il y a beau temps que nous trouvions naturel qu'une lice nourrit un jeune chat, qu'une chatte choisît, pour dormir, le dessus de la cage où chantaient des serins verts confiants et qui, parfois, tiraient du bec, au profit de leur nid, quelques poils soyeux de la dormeuse. (*O*, 1:1000)

> [I was not surprised at the chain of mutually sucking cats. To those who live in the country and use their eyes, everything becomes alike miraculous and simple. We had long considered it natural that a bitch should nourish a kitten, that a cat should select as her lair the top of the cage wherein trustful green canaries sang happily, their beaks from time to time plucking from the sleeper an occasional silky hair for nesting purposes.] (50)

Again, the plurality of creatures interacting in miraculous, polyvalent ways is thematically foregrounded.

The lesson is then repeated by a childhood reminiscence of collecting live flies to feed two young swallows cast into this domestic space by an autumn storm:

> C'est grâce à elles que je sais combien l'hirondelle apprivoisée passe, en sociabilité insolente, le chien le plus gâté. Les deux nôtres vivaient perchées

sur l'épaule, sur la tête, nichées dans la corbeille à ouvrage, courant sous la table comme des poules et piquant du bec le chien interloqué, piaillant au nez du chat qui perdait contenance . . . Elles venaient à l'école au fond de ma poche, et retournaient à la maison par les airs. (O, 1:1000)

[It was thanks to them that I learned how infinitely a tame swallow can surpass, in insolent sociability, even the most pampered of dogs. Our two swallows spent their time perching on a shoulder or a head, nestling in the work-basket, running about the table like chickens, pecking at the non-plussed dog or chirping in the very face of the disconcerted cat . . . They came to school in my pocket and returned home by air.] (51)

The multiplicity of possible bonds of affection is thus exponentially increased by such a plurivalent, multispecies household, where dogs, cats, birds, and humans interact in countless different, "miraculous and simple" ways.

Colette goes on to describe the swallows coming swift as "arrows" to her call, alighting in her hair, "to which they would cling with all the strength of their little curved black steel claws" [cramponées de toutes leurs serres courbes, couleur d'acier noir] (O, 1:1000/51). Further examples of this magical environment are adduced, such as Babou, the cat who loved to eat strawberries and who could be found "poetically absorbed in smelling newly-opened violets" [qui respirait, poétique, absorbé, des violettes épanouies] (O, 1:1000/51), or the spider "kept" by her mother, who would wait a certain hour to descend from its web high above the parental bed down to the bowl of chocolate on the nightstand, where, "grasping the edge of the cup with all eight legs, she would bend over head foremost and drink to satiety" [empoignait de ses huit pattes le bord de la tasse, se penchait tête première, et buvait jusqu'à satiété] (O, 1:1001/52), before climbing back slowly to her ceiling lair. The special role of the mother in orchestrating this multifarious menagerie of a home is glimpsed in this portrayal of the "pet" spider and is rendered manifest when "Sido" shows off to her returning daughter a caterpillar ready to become a chrysalis after having been nursed back to health in the wake of an injury: "A bird must have pecked her stomach but she's quite well again now" [Qu'un oiseau avait dû blesser au ventre, mais elle guérie] (O, 1:1001/53). In response to the daughter's concern over the caterpillar's voraciousness, its ability to eat anything and everything, not just the irksome box thorn but the beloved honeysuckle as well, the mother answers with feigned perplexity: "Je ne sais pas . . . Mais que veux-tu que j'y fasse? Je ne peux pourtant pas la tuer, cette bête" [I don't know. But in any case, what can I do about it? I can hardly kill the creature] (*O*, 1:1002/53). The tolerance and love of life, in all its miraculous diversity, is inevitably subsumed and expressed in the figure of the mother, whose boundless generosity makes such a polymorphous world possible. As for the daughter, now nearly fifty herself, who writes with "all this still before my eyes" [Tout est encore devant mes yeux] (1:1002), her task is to provide at long last the following:

> pour accompagner dignement la voix qui a dit ce jour-là, et tous les autres jours jusqu'au silence de la fin, des paroles qui se ressemblaient:
> "Il faut soigner cet enfant . . . Ne peut-on sauver cette femme? Est-ce que ces gens ont à manger chez eux? Je ne peux pourtant pas tuer cette bête . . ." (*O*, 1:1002)

> [a worthy accompaniment to the voice that on that day and on all other days, even to the final silence, spoke words that had always the same meaning:
> "That child must have some proper care. Can't we save that woman? Have those people got enough to eat? I can hardly kill the creature."] (53)

"Sido" in Colette's mature writing (and after the publication of *La maison de Claudine,* she begins to sign all her works simply as "Colette") thus becomes the name for the matriarchal utopia of the childhood home and everything that makes such a feminocentric world imaginable. In a very late text significantly titled "Des mères, des enfants" (Mothers and Children), published only in 1949 as part of her *Oeuvres complètes,* Colette revisits the domestic paradise of the Puisaye home, once again underscoring the proliferating variety of living creatures, predominantly female and endlessly reproducing themselves as daughters in turn becoming the mothers of other daughters:

> Des mères, des enfants; des lices, leurs chiots, les chattes, les chatons à raison de douze par tête, ou mieux par ventre des chatte; la vache Violette, son veau qu'on lui enleva; les hirondelles, qui pour capitonner leur nid enlaçaient, au duvet des poules, quelques-uns de mes longs cheveux; la portée d'une souris, six souriceaux gros comme des frelons, tétant tous à la fois leur mère minuscule . . . Peu de mâles; de temps en temps un interminable matou, noir comme l'anguille mouillée, un chien trouvé, un limier, offert en cadeau, et que nous n'avions pas osé refuser . . . Des mères, des rejetons, féconds à leur tour: voilà qui ne m'a jamais manqué, pendant les vingt premières années de ma vie. Ainsi le voulait l'ordre des choses, aussi fatal que le fil d'une rivière. Pensais-je moins à ma propre mère qu'à toutes ces mères qui m'entouraient? C'est possible. On ne songe pas à la présence de l'air. (*OC*, 14:341)

[Mothers and children; bitches and their puppies; female cats and their kittens, a dozen or so per head or, rather, per cat belly; the cow Violette, her calf that was taken away from her; swallows that lined their nest with chicken down laced together with some of my long hairs; the litter of mice, six tiny ones the size of wasps, all being suckled at once by their tiny mother . . . There were a few male animals. Now and then there was an interminable tomcat, black as a wet eel, and a stray dog, a bloodhound offered us as a gift which we dared not refuse . . . But mothers and their offspring, in their turn fertile! There was never any lack of these during the first twenty years of my life. Thus was the natural order of things, as inevitable as the course of a river. Did I perhaps think less about my own mother than about all these mother creatures surrounding me? Perhaps. We never think about the presence of the air.][13]

Sido stands behind this feminist utopia as its very substance, the ground on which it stands or the very air of its atmosphere. She so powerfully permeates and embraces the entirety of her household that in the eyes of her child she is as invisible as the force of nature itself. Colette's Sido, divine protectress of women and animals, is thus the epitome of the Artemisian ideal, the true Diana who watches over that domestic space where reigns an intimacy more intimate than love itself, what Colette describes in the following passage as "une paix profonde de gynécée" (the profound peacefulness of a gynaeceum):

Et je me mis en boule aux pieds de "Sido," la tête à la hauteur de ses genoux. Le soleil de trois heures me ferma les paupières, et le va-et-vient du peigne m'engourdit. Au creux d'un fauteuil d'osier dormait une chatte pleine; en étandant la main je tâtais son flanc habité, les têtes rondes de la portée prisonnière et ses bonds de dauphins sous le flot. Bienheureuse, la chienne bâtarde allaitait ses bâtards, croisés de chiens d'arrêt et de demi-grifonne. Points de garçons adolescents en vue, point d'homme. Des mères, des enfants encore ignorants de leur sexe, une paix profonde de gynécée, sous les nids de mai et la glycine transpercée de soleil. Je ne tenais plus au monde réel que par le ronronnement de la chatte, le clair tintement d'une enclume proche, et les mains de ma mère, qui sur ma nuque légèrement tressaient mes cheveux. (OC, 14:346)

[And I curled up at the feet of Sido, my head at her knees. The three-o'clock sunlight crossed my eyelids and the to-and-fro movement of the comb made me drowsy. In the depths of a rattan armchair slept a pregnant cat; stretching out my hand, I felt her inhabited flanks, the round heads of the imprisoned litter, and its dolphin leaps beneath the flood. Blissful, the mongrel bitch suckled her mongrel pups, a mixture of pointer and griffon and heaven knows what. No adolescent males anywhere, no sign of a man. Mothers. Children still ignorant of their sex. The profound peacefulness of a gynaeceum, under the nests of May and the wisteria shot with sunlight. I was no longer linked with the real world except by the purring of the cat, the clear ringing of a nearby anvil, and the hands of my mother at the back of my neck, deftly braiding my hair.] (35–36; translation modified)

But while the many-specied daughters sleep, the divine mother remains vigilant, ready to sever, to wean or to exclude those whose presence is better sent elsewhere:

> Car je n'ai pas pu ne pas remarquer, dès mon jeune âge, que la mansuétude de "Sido," épandue sur les nouveau-nés, tous les nouveau-nés, sur les mères anxieuses près de leur terme, ne remontait pas jusqu'au géniteur. Elle avait une mordante manière de rabaisser la fatuité des jeunes pères, béats au chevet d'une accouchée exsangue. Moffino, notre chien de chasse, fut vertement relevé de la garde bénévole qu'il montait près d'une corbeille pleine de petits chiens:
> —Mais, maman, ce sont ses enfants! pleurnichai-je.
> Sur le visage de ma mère brilla cette gaîté impénétrable et combative qui souvent me déconcertait.
> —Justement, dit-elle.
> —Pauvre Moffino, reniflai-je, où veux-tu qu'il aille?
> —Où l'appelle son rôle de père, riposta ma mère. Au café. Ou bien jouer aux cartes avec Landre. Ou bien faire de l'oeil à la lingère. (*OC*, 14:345)

[However, I could not help remarking from my very early years that Sido's kindness lavished upon the newborn, all and any newborn, and upon anxious mothers nearing their time, did not extend to the progenitor. She had a cutting way of puncturing the fatuity of young fathers who blissfully sat at the side of a weakened young mother in childbed. Moffino, our hunting dog, was roughly relieved of the benevolent guard he was keeping beside a basket full of puppies.
"But, Mamma, they're his children!" I sobbed.
On my mother's face sparkled that impenetrable and combative gaiety that so often disconcerted me.
"Exactly," she said.
"Oh, poor Moffino," I sniveled, "where can he go?"
"Wherever his role as father takes him," retorted my mother. "To the tavern. Or to play cards with Landre. Or to flirt with the washerwoman."] (35)

The lesson behind this humorous conflation of dog and husband is clear and recalls the place of the tomcat/lover in "Nonoche": that the males are tolerated for a limited time only, perhaps not even any longer than the time for breeding.

The tale of "Nonoche," in this context, can then also be seen as portraying two different territories outside Colette's idealized domestic space: on the one side, the undomesticated world of wild beasts or "fauves"; on the other, the far more savage world of men and their "civilization." These dystopic but all-too-real outlands to the alternative world of Sido and her animals become the object of intense reflection throughout Colette's work as it continues to develop. The short tale of "Nonoche," with its analytical depiction of the perils of passion, can be seen in this sense as already bearing the kernel of Colette's great love novels—*L'entrave, Chéri, Le blé en herbe, La fin de Chéri, Duo*—where she dissects the awesome, even fatal, vicissitudes of human desire and, as prefigured in *Les vrilles de la vigne*, the unpredictably entangling effects of the affective bond.

A parallel set of reflections addresses the pathos of the animal in its relation with human beings, the poignant adaptations of beasts to such human inventions as warfare and cities, the unperceived tribulations of animals in domestic service, circus performances, or scientific experiments. Most appalling for Colette was their institutionalized exhibition in zoos, which distressed her so much that she once applied for a zoo director's job to try to improve conditions for the captive beasts. In such late pieces as "Amertume" and "Leurs petits et les nôtres," Colette, not content just to denounce obvious abuses or the inhumane treatment of animals, raises the ethical issues involved in treating nondomestic animals like domestic ones and confining them to domestic spaces. Here she speaks with the authority of someone whose own experiences with animals, as depicted in her short stories, are extraordinarily diverse. If part of the pleasure of a domestic menagerie like Sido's is the exploration of very *different* kinds of bonds or affective relations with *different* kinds of living creatures, that pleasure—love—demands a recognition of the alterities implied in those bonds and, indeed, the limit of the bonds (again, the lesson of Nonoche). Colette's stories on this subject range from the comical (as in her account of Poucette, the mendacious dog, or Pati-Pati, the little Brabancon who dislikes other animals) to the tragic, as in her description of Bâ-Tou, the wild tiger-cat from Chad, whom Colette was at last obliged, despite her own contrary inclinations, to donate to a zoo in Rome. One of the final chapters in *La maison de Claudine* is an eloquent and emotional elegy to this beautiful animal, a true "fauve" foreign to all human civilization:

> Je n'avais jamais possédé, dans ma maison, une créature aussi naturelle. La vie quotidienne me la révéla intacte, préservée encore de toute atteinte civilisatrice. Le chien calcule et ment, le chat dissimule et simule. Bâ-Tou ne cachait rien. . . .

Quand je vous regrette, Bâ-Tou, j'ajoute à mon regret la mortification d'avoir chassé de chez moi une amie, une amie qui n'avait, Dieu merci, rien d'humain. . . .

Hélas! Bâ-Tou, que la vie simple, que la fauve tendresse sont difficiles, sous notre climat . . . Le ciel romain vous abrite à présent; un fossé, trop large pour votre élan, vous sépare de ceux qui vont, au jardin zoologique, narguer les félins; et j'espère que vous m'avez oubliée, moi qui, vous sachant innocente de tout, sauf de votre race, souffris qu'on fît de vous une bête captive. (O, 2:1064)

[I have never kept in my house a creature as natural as she. Living with her day by day showed me how intact she was, how preserved from any civilizing reach. The dog calculates and lies, the cat dissimulates and simulates. Bâ-Tou hid nothing. . . .

When I miss you, Bâ-Tou, I add to my regret the mortification of having cast a friend out of my home, a friend who, thank God, had nothing human about her. . . .

Alas! Bâ-Tou, how a simple life and beastly tenderness are hard in our climate . . . The Roman sky shelters you now; a ditch, too wide for you to leap, separates you from those who go to the zoo to jeer the big cats; and I hope you have forgotten me, I who, knowing how innocent you are about everything, except about your race, allowed you to be made a captive animal.][14]

In the collection of stories and sketches called *Prisons et paradis* (1932), "Ecureuil" describes another wild animal, Pitiriki the squirrel, who is given to her as a gift but whose suffering in the captivity of the home ultimately leads her, with many misgivings, to "inflict" his freedom upon him (O, 3:667).[15] At first remaining close by, he becomes increasingly adventurous yet faithfully returns home every night, until "one night, Pitiriki did not come home, nor any other night":

La main humaine, j'en suis sûre, s'était de nouveau abbatue sur lui, sur son doux pelage, ses élastique pattes postérieures faites pour le long saut plané, ses oreilles qu'il pliait latéralement pour offrir son crâne à la caresse.

C'est en pensant à Pitiriki, à quelques autres bêtes dépaysées parmi nous, amèrement claustrées, que je me sens si souvent "méchante à l'homme" (O, 3:666)

[Human hands, I am sure, bore down again upon him, upon his soft pelt, his elastic, back paws made for long, gliding jumps, his ears which he folded laterally to let his skull be pet.

It is when I think of Pitiriki, and to some other animals dislocated among us, bitterly confined, that I feel myself become "mean to man."]

And, in the same collection, "Lézard" tells another story of a bond that could not take hold: a lizard saved from the cat's jaws is nursed back to health in the best tradition of Sido and given affection but, when given a chance to reciprocate, disappears with lightning speed into the bush. The ultimate lesson of these stories and many, many others like them penned by Colette is again that of the wild animal, like the tomcat in the shadows, whose essence is its wildness and whom it is our obligation as humans *not* to bring into our domestic enclosures of whatever kind.

Some humans opt to go over to the wild to escape a worse fate among men, such as the abused women Colette describes in "Cavernes" (*OC*, 14:428–32), who hide themselves and their children in caves and other forsaken places, living a life like that of "wolves, foxes," or "stray cats" (*OC*, 14:428), or the invisible inhabitants of Parisian parks, resourceful in their homelessness, as described, for example, in "Plein air" (*Journal à rebours, OC*, 12:115). Alternatively, there is the dangerous passion humans seem to elicit in animals, leading them to place all their trust in human beings, even to their own detriment. One wonders, then, to whom the word *wild* applies:

> C'est l'homme qui a accolé, au nom de la bête, le mot "sauvage." Demandez là-dessus leur avis à ceux qui vécurent solitaires, qui forcèrent un domaine, encore inviolé, de la bête. Interrogez le trappeur que l'ours ménage et suit, le chasseur que la clémence du fauve et ses jeux condescendants surprirent. Ceux-là vous apprendront sans doute que nous sommes l'éternelle curiosité, la passion malheureuse de toutes les bêtes, leur climat décevant, gonflé d'orages. Si elles goûtent à notre intempérie quotidienne, elles en demeurent nostalgiques à jamais. ("Bêtes," *Aventures quotidiennes, O,* 3:93–94)

> [Man it is who has connected the word *wild* to the name of the beast. Ask those who have lived alone, who have broken into an as yet inviolate animal lair, what they think of this. Ask the trapper whom the bear carefully deals with and follows, the hunter whom the clemency of the beast and its condescending games surprised. They will undoubtedly teach you that we are the eternal curiosity, the unfortunate passion of all animals, their deceptive climate, swollen with storms. If they get a taste of our daily intemperateness, they remain forever nostalgic for it.]

Despite the rampant savagery and cruelty of humans, animals display a boundless trust and an "unmerited faith" (*O,* 3:91) in them, resembling in their patient suffering abused women: "Sous la colère incompréhensible de l'homme, si l'une gémit, pure de haine: 'Ah! quel mauvais temps!', l'autre soupire, avec la gratitude désespérée d'une amante qu'on rudoie: 'Ça vaut encore mieux que pas du tout . . .'" [Under the incomprehensible anger of man, if one groans, full of hatred: "Oh! What awful weather!," the other sighs, with all the desperate gratitude of a browbeaten mistress: "This is still better than nothing at all . . ."] (O, 3:94). The constrictive tendrils of patriarchy are thus transcoded from the relations between the sexes to those between "men" and other species.

And, in a stunning reversal presented with all the "urgency" of a confession, Colette at one point paints herself disturbingly in the role of the tomcat from "Nonoche":

> Il me paraît juste, urgente, que je raconte comment une chatte rayée, que j'avais dû donner à ma mère, courut sur ma trace dans la neige, me chercha pendant cinq jours et quatre nuits, revint épuisée, et ne se soucia guère de son nouveau-né, qu'elle avait laissé mourir . . . Ce n'est pas, bien entendu, de la mort du chaton que je m'enorgueillais. Je cherche pourquoi elle l'a laissé mourir, et pourquoi, ayant accepté de vivre une année sans moi qui voyageais au loin, elle trahit pourtant, rien que de m'avoir revue, sa race et sa descendance . . . ("Le coeur des bêtes,' *Journal à rebours*, OC, 12:106).

> [It appears just and urgent to me that I recount how a striped cat, which I must have given my mother, followed my path in the snow, sought me for five days and four nights, returned exhausted, and gave hardly a thought to its newborn, whom she had allowed to die . . . Obviously, it is not that I took any pride in the death of the kitty. I am searching why she let it die, and why, after having agreed to live a year without me during which I traveled far away, she nevertheless betrayed her race and her progeny for nothing more than having seen me again . . .]

Here the seductive attraction of a human being is so overpowering as to make the mother cat forget everything, her own kitten and her own being and lineage as feline.

Why her pull on the cat is so strong remains an enigma for the narrator ("Je cherche pourquoi"); *that* it is so demands nothing less of a response than the acceptance of this truly miraculous gift of love: "Puisqu'il n'y a pas d'amour sans dommage, j'accepte d'être, dans le coeur du félin, la préférée qu'un passage étroit et brûlant mène jusqu'au coeur du chat" [Since there is no love without loss, I agree to be, within the feline heart, the one who is preferred and whom a narrow and burning passage leads straight to the heart of the cat] (OC, 12:106). To accept this love is to allowed admittance to the very "heart" of the beast, an intimacy of intercourse that concomitantly renders the beloved human suspicious to other humans, just as though she had broken some sacred, unspoken vow that places her on the same footing as the adulteress, the "vagabond," the criminal, or even the cannibal: "Quand je m'en reviens, il arrive qu'on me reçoive ici en exploratrice un peu suspecte. N'ai-je pas, là-bas, mangé mon semblable? Ou pactisé criminellement? Il serait temps que la race stictement humaine s'en inquiétât" [When I return, it happens that I am received as a slightly suspect explorer. Have I not eaten one of my own over there? Or made criminal deals? It's time the strictly human race began to worry] (OC, 12:106). Such figurations of the marginal were, of course, nothing unusual for Colette either in her work or in her life, as her increased acclaim as a writer was not divorced from occasional suspicion cast on her person, with some even going so far as to question whether she had a "soul": "Il serait temps que la race strictement humaine s'en inquiétât . . . De fait, elle s'en inquiète. Sur ma table, un article de journal s'intitule gravement: *Madame Colette a-t-elle une âme?*" [It's time the strictly human race began to worry . . . In point of fact, it has begun to worry. On my table, there is a magazine article gravely titled: *Does Madame Colette have a soul?*]" (OC, 12:106). By her intense closeness to animals, she crosses a line of human tolerance similarly encountered of old by those daughters of Diana, the witches and their familiars.

For the gynaeceum is not just the nostalgic fantasy of Sido and the maternal home, it is also the utopic alternative to patriarchal domesticity and, as such, is to be found more on the side of the beasts than of men. In a key passage from *La naissance du jour* (*Break of Day;* 1928), the second of the three major works reclaiming the world of the mother (after *La maison de Claudine* and before *Sido*), Colette describes the unbridgeable chasm between beasts and men and the scandalous consequences of choosing the former over the latter, consequences so scandalous as to require an unusual discretion and reserve on the part of the author. After a long panegyric to the animal world occasioned by the question, "M'émerveillai-je jamais assez des bêtes?" [Shall I ever marvel enough at animals?] (O, 3:302/43), she makes a startling declaration:

> Mais je n'aime plus écrire le portrait, l'histoire des bêtes. L'abîme, que des siècles ne comblent point, est toujours béant entre elles et l'homme. Je finirai par cacher les miennes, sauf à quelques amis, qu'elles choisiront. Je montrerai les chats à Philippe Berthelot, puissance féline, à Vial, qui est amoureux de la chatte et qui prétend, avec Alfred Savoir, que je puis susciter un chat dans un endroit où il n'y a pas de chat . . . On n'aime pas à la fois les bêtes et les hommes. Je deviens de jour en jour suspecte à mes semblables, je ne leur serais pas suspecte (O, 3:303).

[But I no longer like describing the appearance or writing stories of animals. The passage of centuries never bridges the chasm that yawns between them and man. I shall end by hiding my own creatures except from a few friends, whom they shall choose. I shall show the cats to Philippe Berthelot, himself full of feline power, and to Vial, who is in love with the she-cat and pretends, as does Alfred Savoir, that I can conjure up a cat in a place where no cat exists . . . One doesn't love beasts and men at the same time. I am becoming daily more suspect to my fellows. But if they were my fellows I should not be suspect to them.][16]

To be close to beasts is to be suspicious to humans, not only to choose otherness of species over them but to *be other to them*, to be dissimilar to those with whom one is supposed to be similar ("mes semblables"). Given such a choice between one's "similars" and one's "familiars," the prudent course would be to hide the latter, revealing them only to those humans whom the beasts themselves would choose for their lack of being "strictly" human (Berthelot's "feline power," etc.). Still, even among friends, the suspicion of witchlike abilities hovers in the air, bodying forth in the (mock) claim that the narrator can indeed "conjure up a cat in a place where no cat exists."

But if one cannot love both men and beasts, then unsurprisingly it is in the traditional marriage arrangement that the conflict is most irredeemably expressed: "'Quand j'entre dans la pièce où tu es seule avec des bêtes,' disait mon second mari, 'j'ai l'impression d'être indiscret. Tu te retireras quelque jour dans une jungle.'" ["When I enter a room where you're alone with your animals," my second husband used to say, "I feel I'm being indiscreet. One of these days you'll retire to a jungle."] (O, 3:303/44). Colette herself offers the best explication of her husband's uncomprehending and utterly anthropocentric remarks:

Sans vouloir rêver à ce qui se pouvait cacher, sous une telle prophétie, d'insidieuse—ou d'impatiente—suggestion, sans cesser de caresser l'aimable tableau qu'elle m'offre de mon avenir, je m'y arrête, pour me rappeler la profonde, la logique défiance d'un homme très humanisé. Je m'y arrête comme à une sentence écrite par un doigt d'homme sur un front qui, si l'on écarte le feuillage de cheveux qui le couvre, sent probablement, au flair humain, la tanière, le sang de lièvre, le ventre d'écureuil, le lait de la chienne . . . L'homme qui reste du côté de l'homme a de quoi reculer, devant la créature qui opte pour la bête et qui sourit, forte d'une affreuse innocence. (O, 3:303)

[I keep toying with the agreeable picture of the future this prophecy offers me, though I've no wish to try and fathom what insidious—or impatient— suggestion may have lain behind it; but I dwell on it to remind myself of the deep, logical mistrust that it reveals in a very civilized man. I dwell on it as on a sentence written by the finger of a man on a forehead that, if one pushes aside the foliage of hair that covers it, probably smells, to a human sense of smell, of a lair, the blood of a hare, the belly of a squirrel, a bitch's milk. Any man who remains on the side of men has reason to shrink from a creature who opts for beasts and who smiles, strong in her dreadful innocence.] (44–45)

No one could be more sensitive than Colette to the judgmental character of her husband's statement, and the implicit castigation of her and all those who like her "smell" a bit too much of the beast. Not only is their punishment visibly inscribed on their forehead (a kind of bestial scarlet letter), but their humanity is itself quickly effaced by their assimilation to the category of the monstrous:

> "Ta monstrueuse simplicité . . . Ta douceur pleine de ténèbres . . ." Autant de mots justes. Au point de vue humain, c'est à la connivence avec la bête que commence la monstruosité. Marcel Schwob ne traitait-il pas de "monstres sadique" les vieux charmeurs desséchés et couverts d'oiseaux qu'on voyait aux Tuileries? Encore si'il n'y avait que la connivence . . . Mais il y a la préférence . . . (O, 3:303)

> ["Your monstrous simplicity . . . Your sweetness full of dark places . . ." How true all those phrases were! From the human point of view monstrosity begins where there arises connivance with animals. Did not Marcel Schwob dub "sadistic monsters" those withered old bird-charmers one used to see in the Tuileries covered with birds? Connivance alone would be one thing . . . but there is preference too . . .] (45)

To "connive" with beasts is bad enough in its implication of conspiratorially betraying the human species, but to assert a "preference" for them is to reach the threshold of human acceptability. It is the hidden threat of Titian's *la bella,* not only delighting in the company of pets, children, and servants in the master's absence but overtly declaring a *preference* for their company over his. And here is a threshold where Colette, that great painter of human intimacy, that relentless examiner of her own past, refuses to cross and where she decides to speak no more:

> Je me tairais ici. Je m'arrête aussi sur le seuil des arènes et des ménageries. Car, si je ne vois aucun inconvénient à mettre, imprimés, entre les mains du public, des fragments déformés de ma vie sentimentale, on voudra bien que je noue, secrets, bien serrés dans le même sac, tout ce qui concerne une *préférence* pour les bêtes, et—c'est aussi une question de prédilection—l'enfant que j'ai mise au monde. (O, 3:303; emphasis in original)

[And at this point I shall keep silent. I stop short also when it comes to arenas and menageries. For if I see no objection to putting into the hands of the public, in print, rearranged fragments of my emotional life, it's understandable that I should tie up tight in the same sack, strictly private, all that concerns a *preference* for animals and—it's a question of partiality too—the child whom I brought into the world.] (45)

Having turned so much of her emotional life into her writing, she nevertheless insists upon an undisclosable inner sanctum, the secret place in the furthest recesses of the home, where reigns her unbridled love for her daughter and her animals. That inner sanctum is Diana's grove, Sido's home, the gynaeceum.

And here the writer accuses herself of having troubled the waters of that pure pond, of being an intrusive Actaeon driven by excessive ambition to shine in the eyes of her brothers, and no doubt those of other men:

Dans le coeur, dans les lettres de ma mère, étaient lisibles l'amour, le respect des créatures vivantes. Je sais donc où situer la source de ma vocation, une source que je trouble, aussitôt née, dans la passion de toucher, de remuer le fond que couvre son flot pur. Je m'accuse d'avoir voulu, dès le jeune âge, briller—non content de le chérir—aux yeux de mes frères et complices. C'est une ambition qui ne me quitte pas. (O, 3:304)

[Love and respect for living creatures could be read in my mother's letters and in her heart. So I know where the spring of my vocation lay, a spring that I muddied as soon as I was born through my passion for touching and stirring up the depths lying beneath the pure stream. I accuse myself of having from an early age, not content with loving them, wanted to shine in the eyes of these, my kin and my accomplices. It is an ambition I still have.] (46)

Far from devouring her, though, the beasts are where she finds the possibility of redemption:

"Vous n'aimez donc pas la gloire?" me demandait Mme de Noailles.
    Mais si. Je voudrais laisser un grand renom parmi les êtres qui, ayant gardé sur leur pelage, dans leur âme, la trace de mon passage, ont pu follement espérer, un seul moment, que je leur appartenais. (O, 3:304)

["Then you don't like fame?" Madame de Noailles asked me.
    But I do. I would like to leave a great reputation among those creatures who having kept, on their fur and in their souls, the trace of my passage, madly hoped for a single moment that I belonged to them.] (47)

To be possessed by the beast thus becomes a true alternative to the tedium and constriction of human love within the parameters of a bourgeois and very patriarchal society. Colette describes the fantasy of such an animal possession, as intense and as dangerous as the tomcat's possession of Nonoche, or the pack's frenzied pursuit of Actaeon, in a confrontation with a lioness at a zoo:

> Une pauvre belle lionne, récemment, m'isola, dans le lot de badauds massés devant la grille. M'ayant choisie, elle sortit de son long désespoir comme d'un sommeil, et ne sachant comment manifester qu'elle m'avait reconnue, qu'elle voulait m'affronter, m'interroger, m'aimer peut-être assez pour n'accepter que moi comme victime, elle menaça, étincela et rugit comme un feu captif, se jeta contre ses barreaux et soudain s'assoupit, lasse, en me regardant . . .
> L'ouïe mentale, que je tends vers la Bête, fonctionne encore. Les drames d'oiseaux dans l'air, les combats souterrains des rongeurs, le son haussé soudain d'un essaim guerroyant, le regard sans espoir des chevaux et des ânes, sont autant de messages à mon adresse. Je n'ai plus envie de me marier avec personne, mais je rêve encore que j'épouse un très grand chat. (O, 3:304)
>
> [A poor lioness, a beautiful creature, recently picked me out from the bunch of gapers massed before her bars. Having chosen me she came out of her long despair as out of a sleep, and not knowing how to show that she had recognized me, that she wanted to confront me, to question me, perhaps to love me to the point where she could accept only me as a victim, she threatened, sparked and roared like a captive fire, hurled herself against the bars and then suddenly, wearied, grew drowsy, still looking at me.
> The mental hearing that I can project toward the Beast still functions. The tragedies of birds in the air, the subterranean combats of rodents, the suddenly increased sound of a swarm on the warpath, the hopeless look of horses and donkeys are so many messages addressed to me. I no longer want to marry anyone, but I still dream that I am marrying a very big cat.] (46)

Colette, the privileged recipient of messages from "the beast," assumes the powerful responsibility of accepting that love (whether from Nonoche *or* the tomcat), and the dilemma of acknowledging that difference between her and the beasts, between her and other humans. Conventional marriage has less meaning within this framework than an intense relation with one's cat.

Such is recognizably, of course, the plot of a late novel, *La chatte* (*The She-Cat;* 1933), which remains among Colette's most controversial and misunderstood texts—in part, I suspect, because of critics' almost total neglect of Colette's writing on animals. Indeed, almost all the criticism devoted to Colette is dedicated to the sequence of love stories from the early Claudine novels up through *Gigi*.[17] *La chatte*, though, is the place where the two strands of her work intersect in the story of a failed marriage in the context of a scandalous attachment to one's pet. Colette adds an extra twist by reversing the gender paradigm, since in this novel it is the man, Alain, who is enamored of his female cat and nostalgic for the childhood home and garden overseen by a very Sido-like mother. Camille, whom he marries and tries to live with for the duration of the novel, appears to be more masculine: sporting a bisexual name, she is ambitious, smokes cigarettes, drives their "roadster," and is the one who has secured the couple's lodging on the seventh floor of a modern, high-rise apartment building. By contrast, Alain is passive and withdrawn, more comfortable when alone with his cat, Saha, and his dreams. Tensions in the couple blow sky-high when Camille, left alone with Saha, can contain her jealousy no longer and pushes the cat off the ledge. Miraculously, Saha survives her perilous fall and is found below by Alain, who confronts Camille with her "crime," then abandons his wife and returns home to live in the sole company of cat and mother.

What could pass anywhere else for a classic love triangle, with the addition here of the species difference, seems to have occasioned consternation *precisely* on account of that addition. The double-edged criticisms of Colette's work, typically voiced by traditional male critics, that praise the beauty of her style only to bemoan her choice of subject matter are especially acute in the case of *La chatte*. Writes one contemporary reviewer: "Having read the book with delight, on account of the beauty of the writing, we doubt if we shall open it again because there is so little in it."[18] A later reviewer similarly asserts: "'The Cat' is a brilliant piece of writing but it is a vile story."[19] Another critic, Pierre Bost, lamenting the "odious" and "ridiculous" nature of the characters, adds that "Mme Colette est peut-être le type même de l'antihumanisme."[20]

One wonders, of course, whether these outcries and similar protests about the story's unbelievability and insubstantiality or the characters' superficiality are not, in fact, reactions to Colette's freewheeling revisions of gender (and species) stereotypes. The novel's great difficulty, and the source of seemingly endless contention, has to do with the ambiguity of its point of view. Despite the tendency of many critics to read the narrative through the point of view of one of the characters to the exclusion of the others, there is no textual justification for this practice. For Germaine Beaumont, Alain is pure and Camille is evil, perhaps the only such character in Colette's opus: "Il y a une maudite dans l'oeuvre de Colette, et c'est la jeune femme qui a essayé de tuer la Chatte" (There is one damned person in Colette's opus, and that is the young woman who tried to kill the She-Cat).[21] Joan Hinde Stewart, on the other hand, sees Camille more positively against an unappealingly childish and "obsessed" Alain: "By a stunning tour de force on the part of Colette, the reader sympathizes with the would-be murderess."[22] Elaine Marks, in turn, sees Saha as "the major and most convincing character" in the novel: "But it is only Saha's physical being that differentiates her from the two other important characters in the novel. And given a scale of human values on which the capacity to love, to feel and to understand is near the top, Saha is more human than Camille."[23] Gonzague Truc also echoes this view when he claims that Saha is the only worthwhile character, the only truly "human" one.[24] All such readings fall into this text's major trap: that of espousing only a single character's viewpoint rather than following this most Racinian of Colette's plots as it dispassionately analyzes the impossible triangulation of the strongly delineated characters. Far from being unbelievable, the story depicts how the minor conflicts of daily life in a household slowly build to a point where the parties' incompatibility of character can no longer be contained. As one critic has remarked, "Marriages have foundered for much less than this," referring to Camille's attempted murder of Saha.[25]

The text of the novel itself addresses the issue of unbelievability when Camille, in the final scene, visits Alain at his mother's house in a last-ditch effort to save their marriage. She tries to explain her very real and legitimate feelings of jealousy aroused by the bond between Alain and Saha ("J'ai voulu, moi, supprimer Saha. Ce n'est pas beau, mais tuer ce qui la gêne, ou qui la fait souffrir, c'est la première idée qui vient à une femme, surtout à une femme jalouse . . . C'est normal." [I wanted to eliminate Saha. That's not pretty, but to kill what gets in her way, or makes her suffer, is the first idea that comes to a woman, especially a jealous woman . . . That's normal.] (O, 3:890). She notes that if her rival had been a human female her actions might appear more excusable: "Si j'avais tué, ou voulu tuer une femme par jalousie, tu me pardonnerais probablement" [If I had killed, or wanted to kill, a woman out of jealousy, you would probably forgive me] (O, 3:890). But not only is her attack on the innocent Saha unpardonable ("une petite créature sans reproche, bleue comme les meilleurs rêves, une petite âme" (a little creature beyond reproach, blue like the best of dreams, a little soul) [O, 3:889]), Alain in response actually justifies her fears by *choosing* Saha over her, leaving Camille incredulous: "Une bête! cria-t-elle avec indignation. Tu me sacrifies à une bête! Je suis ta femme, tout de même!

Tu me laisses pour une bête!" [An animal! she cried out in indignation. You're sacrificing me for an animal! I'm your wife, after all! You're leaving me for an animal!] (*O*, 3:889). For Camille, Alain's choice is literally unbelievable (as it is for many a reader of this book!). The very last sentence of the novel underscores this unbelievability, inscribed right into the text itself, as Camille looks back one last time at the other two characters, who have to all intents and purposes exchanged their species identities: "Car si Saha, aux aguets, suivait *humainement* le départ de Camille, Alain à demi couché jouait, d'une paume adroite et creusée *en patte,* avec les premiers marrons d'août, verts et hérissés." [For if Saha, on the lookout, was *humanly* following Camille's departure, a crouching Alain, his palm ready and made hollow *like a paw,* was playing with the first chestnuts of August, green and prickly] (*O*, 3:891; emphasis added). The scandal of such "unhuman" or "antihuman" behavior is, as I have hoped to demonstrate by this study, as unacceptable to other human beings as it is in fact more common than one would think. The charge leveled at the book of being "unrealistic" or implausible or lacking in substance is merely the aesthetic correlative of the moral accusation, to which Colette among others is supremely sensitive, that those who choose animals over humans are traitors to the species and worthy of every abuse (the burning of witches and their familiars, the institutionalization of pathological pet "collectors" in mental hospitals, etc.). Moreover, the possibility of someone choosing animal love over human love has, as we have seen, been long prepared in Colette's opus, well before she wrote *La chatte* at age sixty.

In the final chapter of this work we will confront a version of *La chatte* where cross-species jealousy leads to the ouster of the human female by the beastly one in the final section of Ackerley's *We Think the World of You.* For the battle between Evie and the narrator's cousin is as much a life-and-death struggle as that between Saha and Camille, a struggle out of which one and only one may survive. The real problem would seem to be the impossibility of female solidarity, the radical exclusion of the gynocentric utopia, anytime the domestic space is organized *internally* by a male *structurally* occupying the patriarchal role (even if that male hardly corresponds in psychic terms to the patriarchal ideal). This structural principle then allows us to grasp the various contradictory attitudes and pathologies that make the characters both attractive and repellent. For Camille has every right to be jealous, but she chooses the wrong object upon which to act (Saha rather than Alain). As for Alain, it is less his object choice that is the matter than the narcissistic regression involved in his relation to the love object: that is, the fact that Saha is more of a way to reconnect to the dreamworld of his imaginary than an honest encounter with otherness based in an understanding and recognition of difference. Indeed, the same problem is evidenced by his relation to Camille, herself repeatedly given feline attributes in the text, since it is precisely her differences that he is unable to accept, such his horror at the nonchalance with which she freely inhabits her naked body in his presence or the nausea that grips him upon finding her hairs in the basin. Ultimately, though, if *La chatte* is a story of interfemale jealousy, it is because Camille and the cat have more in common than either they or Alain would like to think. The problem is they are practically obliged to be in competition for the central male's affection, defining this domestic space not as polymorphous but as unidirectionally viro-centric.

We have already seen alternatives to that domestic order, such as the "Nonoche" paradigm, where the male is situated *externally* to the space of the gynaeceum. One might also imagine a domestic space that does not exclude the male but is not organized around him either. Such might be what Colette experimented with in her third and final marriage, to Maurice Goudeket. For while, in *La naissance du jour*, she states her antipathy to marriage, except perhaps to a "big cat," she did indeed marry again: if not a cat, then at least someone who was quite willing to abide her attraction to animals. Together, they acquired the cat who would be Colette's last pet, the animal called only "la Chatte" and later "la Chatte Dernière." According to Goudeket, that cat, "the Cat," was "non seulement le modèle du personnage félin de *La Chatte*, mais encore ce livre n'eût pas été écrit sans elle" (not only the model of the feline character in *The Cat*, but what was more, that book would not have been written without her). But far from representing a point of conflict in their relationship, "the Last Cat" was acquired at a cat show in Paris with all the erotic thrill of an elopement plotted in common: "Nous décidâmes de l'enlever sur l'heure, comme une fiancée."[26]

Fifteen years her junior, Goudeket was as young relative to Colette as Colette in turn had been to her first husband. But if the domineering Willy had made Colette one of his ghostwriters, Goudeket would instead help edit Colette's *Oeuvres complètes*, would write a biography of her, and would take charge of her literary interests, including negotiations with the Willy estate regarding rights to the early *Claudine* novels. In turn, Colette's by now celebrated fame as a writer would protect the Jewish Goudeket himself in his hour of need, as she managed somehow to pry him loose from the Gestapo in early 1942 before he would have been deported to a concentration camp. At the time of her death Colette had become such an icon of French culture that she was given the unusual honor of a state funeral, despite a checkered past that at the same time led the Catholic Church publicly to deny her a Christian burial, and despite her own wish, quoted earlier from *La naissance du jour*, to be remembered only by the beasts who had "kept, on their fur and in their souls, the trace of [her] passage, madly hop[ing] for a single moment that [she] belonged to them" (O, 3:304/47).

Despite the charges of superficiality and of dubious morality leveled against her work, accompanied by backhanded compliments to the beauty of her written style, Colette should be credited as having brought about in the literary world a revolution as quiet as it was effective, one that finally legitimated the polymorphously domestic space of the gynaeceum as a proper space of writing. It was as if Titian's *la bella* could now take up pen and paper and describe her own world, not as a "private" space seen through the eroticized male gaze, but as a very public space where different classes, races, genders, and species could commingle. Colette's last works—*De ma fenêtre, Le fanal bleu, L'étoile vesper, Trois . . . six . . . neuf*—write this domestic space through an undefinable mix of fiction and autobiography that lyrically evokes her daily life, various houses she has lived in, friends she has had, and of course her many dealings with animals. These and especially her "last" pet, "la Chatte," thus stand as a sign for this new literary space that is a celebration of the everyday lyricism of the domestic:

> Quand je cesserai de chanter la Chatte Dernière, c'est que je serai devenue muette sur toutes choses.
>
> [If I ever cease to sing the praises of the Last Cat, it will be when I no longer have anything to say about anything.][27]
>
> Ce que la Chatte ne sait pas ne vaut pas la peine d'être su.
>
> [What the Cat doesn't know isn't worth knowing.][28]

CHAPTER 3

Romancing the Beast

J.R. Ackerley's Dog Days and the Meaning of Sex

Error has made animals into men; is truth perhaps capable of making man into an animal again?
—Friedrich Nietzsche

"I think love is beautiful and important—anyhow I have found it so in spite of all the pain—and it will sadden me if you fail in this particular way."[1] So wrote E.M. Forster to his friend the writer and literary editor J.R. Ackerley, upon Ackerley's apparent turn away from his sexual predilection for young working-class boys and toward a state of total absorption by his dog, Queenie—whom Forster, in an unkind and no doubt somewhat jealous turn of phrase, called "that unnecessary bitch." Having acquired Queenie from an imprisoned ex-lover—the story is told in great detail and with much elegance in his autobiographical novel *We Think the World of You*—Ackerley at the age of fifty did go through a sea change in his lifestyle. He stopped frequenting the young guardsmen he found in pubs off Hyde Park or in Soho, abandoned his lifelong quest for the "ideal friend" of Greek letters, and ended up devoting all his attention to a female German shepherd dog. But does Ackerley's obvious disappointment in his relations with gay lovers and the transfer of his libidinal energy from humans to animals constitute, as Forster suggests, a kind of erotic "failure"? Is Queenie a poor substitute for the impossible ideal of the ideal friend, or is she instead the very fulfillment and realization of that dream in the sentimental form of "man's *best* friend"? In what ways is his relationship with his dog comparable, or not, to his relationships with his previous lovers? I believe an attentive reading of Ackerley's work precludes any easy answers to these questions. Furthermore, a close reading can avoid those twin temptations of Ackerley's critics to engage in either excessive literalism (as in the often-asked question: Did Ackerley have sex with Queenie?) or an equally excessive figurality that simplistically reduces Queenie to a metaphor for one of Ackerley's significant others: his mother, his sister, even his father.[2] Building on insights from the earlier chapters of this study on the multidirectionality of affect in domestic pet keeping, this chapter will consider the libidinal potency of the modern relation between human and animal, a relation for which Ackerley is not just an exemplary case but also one of its primary and most eloquent thinkers.

We Think the World of You is a story about the transfer of affect (indeed, about a whole world of affective changes and exchanges) that traditionally surfaces in early modern court poetry (such as that of Desportes or Ronsard) in the form of a kind of libidinal threat, that the desire for the love object will be transferred to the mediational entity that is the pet or animal associated with the love object: in other words, that the pet may itself be desired as a kind of synecdochal fulfillment for the absent lover, instead of being desired in a way that designates the pet as a potential rival deserving of the lover's deepest jealous suspicions. Ackerley's quasi-fictional novel actualizes this traditional scenario through a set of triangular relations between the narrator, Frank, his ex-lover Johnny, and various family members, including most prominently Johnny's dog, Evie. At the same time, a libidinal dynamics is set in motion by proliferating metaphorical relations between the characters, which lead to the set of transferences that drive the plot.

In the forefront among these is the process by which Frank's affections for Johnny are displaced onto Evie. Arrested for housebreaking (not housebroken?), Johnny is sent off to prison for a year. Unable to care for his young dog, Evie, he asks Frank to take care of her, but Frank immediately refuses. Later, much later, we learn that Johnny in fact stole money to buy Evie after Frank had refused him a loan. And while Johnny's purchase of the puppy is at first presented as a plan to make money by breeding, later we find out that the puppy replaces an earlier "Evie" that was Johnny's childhood pet. This delay in information, not only for the reader but also for Frank, from whose point of view the story is told, is consequential in breaking down the affective bond between Johnny and Evie. Johnny's actions thus appear callous and incoherent, rather than desperate to the point of obsession, while Evie's placement in the working-class home of Millie and Tom (Johnny's mother and her latest man in a string of husbands) and confinement to a tiny outside area can then appear as a case of virtual neglect and abandonment.

Frank's interest in Evie is sparked only by an apparent misidentification *on the dog's part*. Receiving no mail from Johnny and—thanks in some measure to the inmate's jealous and possessive wife, Megan—unable to obtain permission for an official visit to see him in prison, Frank assuages his frustrations somewhat by occasionally visiting Tom and Millie. As Johnny's long-suffering mother, Millie is, of course, an obvious target of Frank's empathetic identification, his companion in loyalty to *and* frustration with the inconstant and now incarcerated Johnny: "She too had suffered many a disappointment over him in the past, and the lovingly prepared supper, put back into the oven to keep hot for him when he was late, had often stayed there all night."[3] She is also the one Johnny turns to after Frank refuses to take his dog. (Ironically, of course, practically the whole plot now turns around the many obstacles Frank encounters in his efforts to reclaim Evie for himself. In fact, he's met with stiff resistance from Johnny's entire family. Ackerley himself apparently still feared reprisals and lawsuits from his ex-lover's family even as the book celebrating his relationship with the dog went to press.[4] And it is in the gloom of a shared sense of absence that Evie makes her first appearance in the novel: "The shadow of Johnny naturally lay somberly upon us all. While we were talking about him, the scullery door was pushed open and a dog came in" (18). Frank quickly finds himself the object of Evie's expansive affections, licks, and kisses, to the point of prompting Millie to exclaim: "P'raps she thinks you're Johnny" (19). Nothing, of course, could be more pleasing to Frank's ears than this remark: "Dear Millie! She often made remarks like this which thrilled me to such an extent that they had upon me almost a physical effect. To be identified with Johnny!" (19). Frank's thrill at Evie's apparent misrecognition comes from the ecstasy of being identified with the object of his own desires. What here occurs as the first step in Evie's seduction of Frank brings Johnny back not through the metonymic proximity of pet to love object so often found in Renaissance love poetry but instead through the metaphoric displacement of *the pet's desire* from the missing love object *onto* the person whose desire is unrequited. This irony, by the way, is intensified by Ackerley's reversal of the names involved, which rewrite the story of his own (Joe Ackerley's) relation with Freddie, as that of Frank with Johnny (J/F:F/J). Rechristening the Queenie of the "real" relation as "Evie," with its transparent allusions to the biblical primal woman-as-temptress, further confirms the peculiar dynamics at work in the story of this transfer of affect from human to beast.

And though Frank's relation to Evie might appear as a form of fetishism, the above scenario makes clear that such is not the case. Far from being the metonymic fantasy substitute for an absence (i.e., the dog as the next best thing to the lost object of desire), Evie is the active agent, who situates Frank, if anything, as *her* fetish by troping the resemblance between him and her absent owner, by means of a metaphor and not by means of the classic Freudian paradigm, metonymy. Evie's act is one of *méconnaissance* and denial. She manages to recathect her libidinal investment in the absent Johnny by directing her affections onto his metaphoric equivalent, Frank. The arrangement works, however, only because Frank is in turn Johnny's frustrated and unrequited lover, whose own erotic energies are diffused as anxiety and nervous obsession with the forces (the prison system, Megan, Johnny's diffidence and passive nonresponsiveness) that place what seem like endless and insurmountable obstacles between himself and Johnny. The physical "thrill" he feels when Millie points out the meaning of Evie's ecstatic welcome is not just, then, the narcissistic pleasure of being the object of another's desire. Rather, it is the seduction of being desired by another who desires him as the object he himself desires. In a convoluted way, then, Evie fulfills Frank's own desire for Johnny: by desiring Frank as Johnny, Evie forces Frank to recognize his own (unfulfilled) desire for Johnny in her affectionate display. To refuse her affections, then, would be to deny the aims of his own desire, and so, in this strange, convoluted way, responding positively to her (as himself desiring Johnny) is also a way to accredit and fulfill his own desire. This complex interactive dynamic of desire recalls, rather than the straightforwardly intrasubjective processes of fetishism, the more intersubjective workings of transference and countertransference, concepts elaborated by Freud as key moments in the libidinal explanation of the talking cure. In the stereotypical situation of analysis, the analysand succeeds in bringing the repressed causes of neurotic behavior into consciousness by "transferring" them and their libidinal cathexes onto the analyst, a lifting of repression or bringing to consciousness that makes it possible for the analysand to work through his or her problem. Part of the wonder and beauty of Ackerley's novel is its staging of such a transferential situation outside the framework of a clinical cure, in the realm of a common (although not altogether quotidian) love story. Obviously, such a psychical event has momentous consequences, as it does for Frank (Joe), who suddenly finds no more reason to chase after young men and settles down to a new life as the jealously guarded possession of his Alsatian bitch. The process *is* the plot of this autobiographical novel. In fact, the novel takes its full length to be worked out and to be realized, but its fundamentals are most marvelously telescoped into that first encounter with Evie. The dog's transferential behavior is not the end of a case history but the beginning of a love story. Disappointed by the distinct lack of ideal qualities in those he sought for his "ideal friend," Ackerley cannot resist the demand to *be* an ideal friend to his dog.

The pleasure Frank takes in being the object of Evie's (his own) desire is ambiguous, for it means not only being her sole possession but also losing his own soul, as we read if we skip to the novel's ending paragraph:

> Since then she has set herself to keep everyone else out of [my life]. None of the succession of visiting helps I engaged to supply my cousin's place stayed longer than a few days; even the sparrows and pigeons that try to perch on my veranda are instantly put to flight; no fly enters and survives; she would know if I stroked another animal on my way home for she smells me all over directly I return and I should suffer from remorse if I hurt her feelings; she cannot actually read my correspondence, but she seizes it all as it falls through the mailbox and tears it to shreds. Advancing age has only intensified her jealousy. I have lost all my old friends, they fear her and look at me with pity or contempt. We live entirely alone. Unless with her I can never go away. I can scarcely call my soul my own. Not that I am complaining, oh no; yet sometimes as we sit and my mind wanders back to the past, to my youthful ambitions and the freedom and independence I used to enjoy, I wonder what in the world has happened to me and how it all came about . . . But that leads me into deep waters, too deep for fathoming; it leads me into the darkness of my own mind. (184)

Strangely, this closing description recalls a scene very early in the novel when he is complaining to Millie about Johnny's excessive attachment to his wife, Megan, whose "true character was instantly revealed [when] she got a legal grip on him . . . and now he can't call his soul his own" (9). Megan here, as elsewhere in the novel, incarnates all too often the terror of the feminine as some kind of demonic possession. A man in the clutches of a woman risks losing everything, up to and including his own soul. It is no wonder that Megan should appear as the most malevolent force in the novel's plot, a diabolical agent whose unscrupulous ruses and preternatural machinations work to keep Frank from Johnnie, and thereby Frank from Evie (since everyone insists he must have Johnny's permission to remove her from Millie's place), as well as Johnny from anyone else, whether that other be Millie, or Frank, or Evie. Only at the very end of the novel does Frank at last come to see that Megan has been working just as hard to keep Johnny all for herself as Evie has been working to get Frank: "The treacherous little Welsh runt of a couple of years ago, how could I help now but regard her as a female of heroic stature, as ruthless, uncompromising and incorruptible as Evie? Both were prepared to fight tooth and nail and to the finish to secure for themselves, and to themselves alone, the love of their chosen male. And both of them won. After a time my cousin retired, broken in health, crushed in spirit, leaving Evie in undisputed possession of my life" (183–84).

That the agents of both Frank's and Johnny's respective loss of soul are "female" is obviously significant in Ackerley's overtly misogynistic view of the degraded domesticity that succeeds a gay bachelorhood. That Ackerley's "girl" is a bitch is doubled by Megan's suspect ethnicity (at least in a British context: "You can't trust the Welsh," warns Tom early on [9]), her characterization as a "runt" (doubling small size with useless animality reminiscent of those Renaissance women's "jewels"), and her implicit reduction to her sexual identity, as a treacherous little cunt. Yet if Frank's attachment to Evie is grounded in the mimetics of his desire for Johnny, what Evie's transference works to bring about in the misogynist "old twank" is a reconsideration of the feminine—and a kind of transferring of values from a certain fear of the feminine and of women to a kind of pleasure in having his soul possessed by a woman. In this way, Evie's (or Queenie's) beastliness makes his own countertransference possible. No simple fetish/phallus, she is a phallic woman penetrating into every recess of his being, ruling over every sector of his life, a true queen.

In fact, the belated tribute to Megan's "heroic stature" comes on the heels of Evie's adamant refusal to compromise and to accept Frank's cousin, Margaret, into their lives. Not that this cousin is any less determined to get Frank for herself. She is, however, prevented from doing so only by a bitch in whom she more than finds her match. The second to the last episode of *We Think the World of You* replays the central plot of the novel. This replay, however, works to motivate or stimulate a shift in the narrator/Ackerley from simple misogyny to radical misanthropy. A patent analogue to Ackerley's sister Nancy, cousin Margaret wants to possess Frank—she "thinks the world" not of Evie but of him (174, 176)—only to be confronted by the even more possessive Evie. Now that Frank is being fought over by two females, he suddenly finds himself in the same position as Johnny; Evie is now in Megan's position (hence his realization about their similarities), and Margaret moves into Frank's role as the intruder. This arrangement confirms the erotic transference by which Frank himself is configured in Johnny's position, thereby fulfilling his own desire for the young guardsman by taking his place. But, of course, in taking Johnny's place, Frank risks the same fate, that of losing his dog. Amused by the squabbles between Evie and Margaret whereby Evie ferociously barks and lunges to prevent the cousin's equally insistent intrusions into Frank's room, Frank nevertheless undergoes a moment of serious panic and terror when Margaret suddenly switches her "tactics" from confronting Evie to trying to woo her away from Frank:

> And now, alas for the lessons of life, alas for human faith, my heart misgave me. Had I prepared my own undoing? I had wanted Evie happy in my absences, and they were becoming longer and more frequent; my cousin was feeding her daily and doing for her all the things I used to do myself; she was seeing far more of her than I. Indeed, it was all as I had desired and planned; excepting that I did not want to lose my dog. When I thought of losing her I trembled with the kind of internal cold that seems the presage of death. I loved her; I wished her forever happy; but I could not bear to lose her. I could not bear even to share her. She was my true love and I wanted her all to myself. I was afflicted, in short, by the same fear that had haunted poor Johnny in his prison, the fear that he might lose his second Evie as he had lost his first. (180–81)

If Ackerley's autobiographical novel is to a large extent a type of *Bildungsroman* in which the narrator learns to recognize and appreciate points of view that at first he finds contemptible or laughable (especially those of women, the working classes, and animals), that realization is not the happy community of Habermassian consensus where dialogue and discussion reveal the fundamental commonality behind different perspectives but the Lyotardian world of divergences and differends, where the lesson is that of multiplicity and the fundamental irreconcilability of different viewpoints. In fact, the communicational gap between humans and animals provides one of the best examples Lyotard gives of what he calls the differend:

> Some feel more grief over damages inflicted upon an animal than over those inflicted upon a human. This is because the animal is deprived of the possibility of bearing witness according to the human rules for establishing damages, and as a consequence, every damage is like a wrong and turns it into a victim *ipso facto*.—But, if it does not at all have the means to bear witness, then there are not even damages, or at least you cannot establish

them.—What you are saying defines exactly what I mean by a wrong: you are placing the defender of the animal before a dilemma. That is why the animal is a paradigm of the victim.[5]

Let us return to Ackerley, for whom the bliss of being (mis)taken for Johnny is also the risk, as we have seen, of losing everything, one's home, one's love object, one's very soul—of losing the kind of liberty Frank wistfully recalls in the novel's last lines, of becoming a prisoner, be it of the law, a relative, or a possessive bitch. The pathos of the struggle with cousin Margaret is not about recovering Frank's freedom but about who will possess his soul and home:

> I hardly remember for how long these two formidable females, the hairy and the hairless one, struggled for my possession. It was certainly more than a year. Naturally it was rather distracting; it was also extremely instructive. I perceived that the intolerable situation from which I had escaped in Johnny's house was being reproduced in my own, though with a difference. The difference, of course, and it was an undeniable improvement, was that I was now the subject instead of the object of jealousy. Poor Margaret was the latter, and it did not fail to secure for her both my sympathy for her sufferings and my respect for her valor to note that she occupied the odious position I had occupied before. (183)

The question is, of course, whether Evie will be Evie and can be "won over" by the intruder's affection or whether she will also be that "treacherous little Welsh runt" Megan, "a female of heroic stature," "ruthless, uncompromising and incorruptible" (183–84).

In fact, Evie does turn out to be incorruptible, as Frank discovers when he wakes up one night to find her missing from his room. A quick search reveals Evie to be shut up in Margaret's room. And the narrator quickly assumes his own abandonment by his dog: "'This is the end,' I thought. 'She loves my cousin more than me. I can never care for her again. I am alone in the cold, cruel world.'" (181). But then, upon hearing "like the sorrow of a ghost, the faint whistling sigh she made through her nose when she was grieving" (181), he goes back to his cousin's door, opens it, and releases the trapped pooch: "She had not been on my cousin's bed, she had been lying by the door; my cousin had enticed and shut her in against her will. I knew then that she was my dog for ever and ever, and I fell asleep with the peacefulness of a child" (181). From this moment on, Evie's success in securing Frank for herself alone and Frank's security in Evie's love for him are as assured as is Margaret's defeat: "After a time my cousin retired, broken in health, crushed in spirit, leaving Evie in undisputed possession of my life" (184). Of course, it can be argued that Frank's position as the undisputed object of Evie's affections is never in question, since the place Frank holds is not that of Johnny per se but that of the *desire* for Johnny. Johnny is never abandoned by either Evie or Frank, but their joint desire for him is assuaged in the bond established between friend and dog. From a libidinal point of view, their fidelity to Johnny never wavers insofar as their mutual affection is a way to pursue their own desires for Johnny, who is not so much abandoned by dog and friend as abducted or diverted, first by the law, then by Megan. Evie's ferocious defense of her man against the intruding cousin, insofar as she thus comes to resemble the equally dauntless Megan, inscribes that action as itself being the culmination of her desire for Johnny/Frank. Indeed, it may be Frank's misrecognition to think that the dog's desire is directed to him, as Johnny situates her in his place rather than Megan's.

Where Johnny stands in all this, however, is not nearly as clear, especially since we are treated only to Frank's first-person narration. Still, enough clues and hints are given to reconstruct another version of the story, one that is much less flattering to the narrator's description of his actions as the generous, heroic rescue of a beautiful beast from deprivation and neglect. This heroic narrative is supported by Ackerley's classism (at least as pronounced if not even more pronounced than his sexism) and the narrator's fantasy projection of Evie as downtrodden nobility and a damsel in distress: "Wolf, fox, great cat, she had an extraordinary dignity, the dignity of a wild beast, the dignity of an aristocrat. Her incongruity in this tiny working-class kitchen was quite shocking" (46). Like a princess of old, fallen on bad times and unrecognized in her surroundings, Evie calls out to some chivalrous suitor to save her. Conversely, it is not just Evie's own owners but all working-class keepers of dogs who are maligned concerning their ignorance and cruelty, as the following passage from Ackerley's diary reveals:

> How irritating and unsatisfactory the so-called working classes are seen to be, with their irrationalities, and superstitions, and opinionatedness, and stubbornness, and food foibles, and laziness, and selfishness, the more one knows of them. Think of them—for one example—with their dogs! If I were a dog, God shield me from a working-class master, like Freddie or anyone else. We know what sort of a life poor Queenie had with his mother and then with him. They had no real feeling for or understanding of her at all. No sympathy. A dog to them is something between a slave, a plaything and a protector. Its character—what it may need to develop that character—never occurs to them. All dogs are the same, big or small. Their diet has nothing to do with what vets recommend—what working-class man would bother

to go to a vet to ask advice?—or what the dog would seem to fancy—but is conditioned by various superstitions and scraps of folklore picked up in pubs, and ignorant opinions of all sorts. "What's good enough for me is good enough for my dog." "Never give a dog raw meat, it makes them savage." "A Bob Martin a day keeps the vet away." "Cigarette ends are good for worms." "Every dog needs worming once a month." . . . and so on. Poor blessed dogs—entirely at the mercy of these ignorant people who think they know everything.[6]

Such intemperate views of the working classes offer an interesting insight into Ackerley's (or his narrator Frank's) sexual interest in young men of that class, precisely the kind of men so roundly put down in this passage. In a sense, Evie/Queenie motivates the sexual turn in Ackerley/Frank's life by fulfilling the fantasy of finding a true diamond in the rough (literally stamped on her forehead as the "diamond-shaped" pattern of her fur markings, which Frank had earlier interpreted as a "Hindu caste mark" [29]), as opposed to his inevitable disillusionment from the discovery that the imagined nobility of the working-class boys was no more than skin deep. The erotic/abject thrill of consorting with those below his social status is suddenly overturned and displaced by the encounter with a being whose manifest superiority is incontestable (via significant markings, pedigree, and anthropomorphized "dignity") and therefore infinitely capable of maintaining the phantasm of a hidden nobility.

The class basis of Frank's desire for Johnny and fascination with Evie also blinds him to the complexity of Johnny's interest in Evie, the details of which emerge only toward the end of the novel when Frank has a conversation with Johnny shortly prior to his release from prison. The first surprise is that Johnny did not receive Evie as a gift but went out and bought her. As he tells Frank "with a grin," "It was the first thing I done when I'd made a bit of money screwin'. Of course I didn't tell *them* that, for they knew I didn't 'ave the cash, so I said she was give me" (147, emphasis in original). Using his "screwin'" money for a down payment, he then breaks into a house to steal the rest—the incident, of course, that triggers the plot—after having unsuccessfully asked his dear friend Frank for a loan. Why this extraordinary recourse to buy a dog? Johnny tells Frank; "I wanted 'er. I saw 'er in a shop winder, and I meant to 'ave 'er. . . . I'm mad on them dogs, didn't you know? I 'ad one when I was a kid. Didn't Mum tell you? I thought the world of 'er, I did. 'Er name was Evie too. I done me nut when she died. She 'ad something wrong with 'er insides. Oh I done me nut! You ask Mum.

I wouldn't eat. I never ate for days. Oh, I went mad! Mum'll tell you" (148). Oddly, Frank seems to have had no inkling of Johnny's dog-craziness, or any suspicion that Johnny's attachment to Evie was senselessly grounded in nostalgia and the return to childhood. If Evie's bond to Frank begins out of a moment of *misprision* (her thinking Frank is Johnny), Johnny's attachment to Evie is similarly motivated by a desire to recover the loss of the first Evie, an impossible aim glossed over by the identity of the signifier that marks both dogs' names.

Frank's inability to perceive the irrationality of Johnny's passion is no doubt motivated by the fact that his own passionate relation to Johnny, as to other young guardsmen, is mediated by money in exchange for sexual favors. And indeed, Frank can explain Johnny's relation to Evie only by asking how much he paid for her. Johnny's answer:

> "I give fifteen quid for 'er. She's good, she is. I mean to breed from 'er when I get out." Then he added: "Megan told me you wanted to buy 'er, Frank. But I wouldn't sell 'er. I've thought of 'er every day since I've been in 'ere. Every day! I wouldn't sell 'er to no one, not for nothing. I wouldn't sell 'er for a thousand pounds!"
>
> "That's all right, Johnny. I wasn't going to ask again. But you'll never be able to keep her. You've no idea. She's a wild beast." (148)

The quibbling over the pricey and the priceless thematizes the rivalry over who will ultimately possess Evie. In answer to Frank's question, Johnny cites the amount she cost, but as if to justify the price he tries to position her, in the eyes of his social superior, as an investment, as if breeding a pup bought out of a store window would make him wealthy and perhaps even the class equal of his friend. But after the relative value of the dog is established, Johnny withdraws her from any conceivable economic exchange and instead insists on her absolute personal value to him: "I've thought of 'er every day since I've been in 'ere. Every day! I wouldn't sell 'er to no one, not for nothing. I wouldn't sell 'er for a thousand pounds!" Retracting previous offers to buy the dog, Frank's answer only seems conciliatory, as he subtly situates the dog beyond the reach of money itself: "You'll never be able to keep her. You've no idea. She's a wild beast." In fact, for Frank, as we have seen and shall see again, it is precisely the beastliness of the dog that qualifies her worth as being beyond the quotidian world of breeding and exchange and defines her *nobility*: "She had an extraordinary dignity, the dignity of a wild beast, the dignity of an aristocrat" (46). Even though Frank acknowledges Johnny's attachment to Evie, he desires to keep her at all costs and removes her to a place beyond Johnny's reach, although significantly, not beyond his own.

Later, after Johnny's release, the two friends have another conversation that throws Evie's situation in another light and makes the class-bound differend between Frank and Johnny even more stark. Again, Frank is caught off-guard by Johnny's perspective:

> "I'm not saying you're wrong about all this, Frank. I'm not saying that. But there's two ways of looking at it."
> "Oh, Johnny," I said, "I'm sure there are. But looking at what?"
> "Well, it's like this. If I 'adn't got nicked screwin' and Evie 'ad lived with me as my dog, she'd 'ave 'ad a different life from what she's 'ad with you, if you see what I mean; but that's not to say she wouldn't 'ave been just as well."
> "I suppose that would depend upon the kind of life you gave her."
> "No, it wouldn't. Not to my way of thinking. That's what I mean. Whatever it was, she'd 'ave got used to it and been just as well off."
> I turned this over in my mind.
> "As happy?"
> "Yes, as 'appy. What you've never 'ad you never miss." (166)

Before Frank's initial resistance to what he sees as Johnny's "determin[ation] to make nonsense of the past," Johnny explains:

> "It's all what you're used to, see? Of course it wouldn't do now, because she's 'ad a different way of life and she'd miss it. But if she'd 'ad my way instead, she'd 'ave been just as 'appy, for she wouldn't 'ave known no better . . . What I mean is, 'ow many dogs, town dogs, gets as much exercise as Evie gets? Not one in a 'undred. Not one in a thousand. Now do they? Lots of them, never do no more than sit about outside the shops and 'ouses they belong, yet you can't say they're un'appy, for they don't know nothing else, and you can't say they're un'ealthy, for they grows old like any other dog what's 'ad a different life." (167–68)

While Frank is quite right finally to understand that it is a question of "his world, not ours," he still does not fully appreciate the different strictures that apply in each. He and Evie may be "required to fit, patient and understanding," into that world, not so much because of Johnny's forcefulness or ability to impose his own priorities over others, but rather because of his world, the working-class world on the edge of survival, in which all beings are required to "fit" or face even worse consequences, the world where, as Marx classically put it, one's value is no more than that of one's labor power—and where alternatives to the regimentation and subsistence wages of industrial work are not to be found, except, perhaps, in a poor soldier's nostalgic quest for a dog symbolic of childhood and its as yet unlimited possibilities, a quixotic quest that can end only in the failure of an incarceration forcibly "fitting" him into the physical strictures of the prison cell. "You 'ad the best of the bargain," Johnny says to Frank in the last words he speaks in the text, expressing his inevitable bitterness toward the man whose wealth and leisure make it possible to give his dog a "better life." If Frank misses part of the lesson, it is to the extent that the differential treatment of working-class dogs and their upper-class equivalents is no more and no less than an allegory of class difference itself.

Frank may have gained his beloved, wild, and noble Evie, but this gain comes at the cost of understanding that his "rescuing" her may not have been as noble or as heroic as he believes it to have been:

> I found myself afflicted by a despondency which had nothing to do with the perception that I had been put, to a large extent, in the wrong. Say what one might against these people, their foolish frames could not bear the weight of iniquity I had piled upon them; they were, in fact, perfectly ordinary people behaving in a perfectly ordinary way, and practically all the information they had given me about themselves and each other had been true, had been real, and not romance, or prevarication, or the senseless antics of some incomprehensible insect, which were the alternating lights in which, since it had not happened to suit me, I had preferred to regard it. . . . Their problems, in short, had been real problems, and the worlds they so frequently said they thought of each other apparently seemed less flimsy to them than they had appeared to me when I tried to sweep them all away. It was difficult to escape the conclusion, indeed, that, on the whole, I had been a tiresome and troublesome fellow who, for some reason or other, had acted in a manner so intemperate that he might truly be said to have lost his head; but if this sober reflection had upon me any effect at all, it produced no feeling that could remotely be called repentance, but only a kind of listlessness as though some prop that had supported me hitherto had been withdrawn. (150–51)

With this realization comes a recognition of the humanity of the working class rather than what he could earlier understand only as "the senseless antics of some incomprehensible insect." But regarding Johnny in particular, Frank painfully realizes that with all his intrusions on behalf of the dog—goodhearted as his concerns for her well-being may have been—he "had managed somehow to despoil him of his possessions at a moment when he had been powerless to defend them. His possessions or, less concedable, more outrageous, some part of himself that he did not wish to give, something that his heart had been unwilling any longer to submit" (165–66). This innermost part of Johnny is the part that is willing to rob and steal to buy a dog named Evie and perhaps return to a time before he was "required to fit, patient and understanding," into the world to which he belongs. Truly, if anyone does appear as a tragic figure in the novel it is Johnny. He loses all around: the love of his dog, the love of his son Dickie, which is taken by his grandparents, his relationship with Frank, and anything or anyone else except the support of his wife Megan (but then, this is also what happens to Frank and Evie, with the important difference that Evie leads Frank further back into the "darkness of [his] own mind" while Johnny loses that "part of himself that he did not wish to give." A significant sign of Johnny's resignation appears at the moment that Frank gets his way with Evie: "After all that I had done for her, and for him, it would have been difficult for him to refuse; what difficulty there was lay in telling, from the quiet 'Okay, Frank' with which he let me have my way, what his true feelings were" (162–63). Although it does become apparent that Johnny does indeed love Evie and that "he thinks the world of her," he loses her as he loses all else. His escalating lack of agency, begun right from the beginning with his incarceration, is the counterpoint to the willed success of those around him, whether Megan or Frank or Evie, all of whom finally succeed in getting what they want at Johnny's expense.

Of course, Johnny's willingness to part with Evie is partly covered and motivated by the failure of that secondary reason for buying Evie: her breeding possibilities. But Evie turns out to be no more the "goldmine of expensive pedigree puppies" (162) than she was the nostalgic return of the earlier Evie. Evie's agency is once again foregrounded as she is described as "hastening" the situation by having "rejected all the pedigree suitors offered her," causing the concomitant suspicion that she is a "barren bitch" (168). The antithesis of Ariosto's fantasy in *Orlando Furioso* of a magical coin-producing dog, Evie is in monetary terms at least a losing proposition. Ultimately, Johnny has no choice but to sell her, since he lacks the means to arrange a breeding during her heyday as a potential brood bitch: "Fees for the hiring of a stud dog were far beyond his means, and what likelihood was there of a boy in his circumstances and neighborhood happening upon someone who owned a suitably blueblooded sire and was willing to lend him for nothing?" (162). Frank, of course, for whom Evie is "as good as gold" and whose own financial situation allows him to indulge in her pure use value without any concerns about exchange or necessary profits, proposes to help Johnny carry out his plans at his (Frank's) own expense: "I would mate her for him, undertaking all the expense, and the proceeds of the litters should belong wholly to him" (162).

Estimated at "about thirty or forty pounds" in her "goldmine period," Evie's value plummets in accordance with her apparent infertility. Still, Frank is more than happy to offer Johnny forty pounds for the dog, a proposition Johnny cannot refuse. (One can only wonder, though, to what extent this economic incentive is foremost in Johnny's mind and whether this is part of Frank's way to feel legitimate in taking the dog away from him, a palliative for that act that would in fact save Johnny from his own poor [delusional] investments—save him from himself, while in the process saving Evie from Johnny and Johnny's family.) As we saw earlier, Frank seems to attach more significance than Johnny does to the breeding issue. In fact, for Johnny, the idea of breeding Evie seems be primarily an excuse for his indulgence in theft and criminality to obtain a creature far beyond his means as well as a source of a purely psychological satisfaction. Frank is the one who proposes ways to arrange the breeding that Johnny is not financially, socially, or psychologically equipped to carry out. All of this raises serious questions about the extent of Johnny's commitment to breeding Evie. Ultimately, he must succumb not only to the financial pressure of maintaining a large dog on a small income but also to the familial pressures of that human counterpart to Evie, the equally possessive and indefatigable Megan, who without a doubt completely understands that getting the dog out of her household is a way of getting her archrival Frank out too: "Now that the dog had passed, I, in Megan's scheme of things could pass also" (173).

We can gain some sense of Frank's motives in maintaining the breeding myth if we ignore the border between fiction and nonfiction and consider some of Ackerley's concerns in *My Dog Tulip,* an earlier work that also gives a view of his relationship with his dog *after* he has successfully acquired her from his lover and family. In fact, though written earlier, *My Dog Tulip* more or less picks up the storyline from where *We Think the World of You* leaves off. The question of breeding the beloved Alsatian turns out to occupy the bulk of the book. In fact, it occupies it entirely except for the first two chapters. And with no mention of the prior owner's (Freddie's) interest in the matter, *My Dog Tulip* is a text driven by the narrator's quest to mate her. But his concerns with breeding the bitch here have no relation to any financial preoccupation; on the contrary, Ackerley remains uniquely involved in meeting what he considers to be Tulip's bodily needs and desires. Furthermore, the two chapters that do not address the question of Tulip's sexuality (the first on her relations with veterinarians, the second, "Solids and

Liquids," on her excretions) already position the question of her body at center stage of the inquiry. The scandal of *My Dog Tulip*, in fact, is its unrepentant celebration (rather than scorn) and treatment of the dog as body, and as a sexed body in particular, as the floral name that he gives to his dog in this book itself suggests: "Soon after Tulip came into my possession I set about finding a husband for her. She had had a lonely and frustrated life hitherto; now she should have a full one. A full life naturally included the pleasures of sex and maternity, and although I could not, of course, accommodate a litter of puppies in my small flat, that was a matter to which I would give my attention later."[7] The operative word in this passage is *frustrated*, and that lexeme comes to provide the conceptual thread to Ackerley's depiction of Tulip's sexual adventures or misadventures. At first glance, it is difficult not to see in this concern of the master for his dog's sexual well-being anything more than an identification and projection of the "aging twank's" own frustrated sexual desires. After all, as we have seen, he acquired the dog in the very course of losing his lover.

The frustration can be further understood to be in relation to what is primarily represented as a physiological need. And the three chapters that constitute the book's core relate, in Ackerley's biting satire, the amazing set of difficulties and obstacles overcome in trying to mate Tulip and raise a litter of her puppies. Disavowing here any "profit-making interest" (59), the narrator begins nonetheless with the viewpoint that "so beautiful a creature as Tulip should certainly have children as pretty as herself" (60) and should accordingly be bred only to another purebred German shepherd. And while in another version of the story Johnny is portrayed as too poor to hire a stud dog and too optimistic in his expectation of meeting a congenial owner of an Alsatian in his own neighborhood, here the narrator, "partly out of thrift" (60), pursues the exact same strategy: "Why pay a fee for hiring a husband when there were quantities of good-looking Alsatians about who might be borrowed for nothing if one got to know their owners? But how does one get to know their owners?" (60). What follows is a series of failed breedings with a variety of purebred suitors, leading once again to the thesis of Tulip's being a "barren bitch." Finally, exasperated by the numbers of males who turn out to be sexually incapable or are simply rejected by Tulip, or both, the narrator finds himself face to face with a possibility that is far removed from his initial intent:

> It was while I stood there, gazing in despair at this exquisite creature in the midst of her desire, that the dog-next-door emerged through what remained

of the fence. He had often intruded before, as often been ejected. Now he hung there in the failing light, half-in, half out of, the garden, his attention fixed warily upon me, a disreputable, dirty mongrel, Dusty by name, in whom Scottish sheep-dog predominated. I returned the stare of the disconcertingly dissimilar eyes, one brown, one pale blue, of this ragamuffin with whom it had always amused Tulip to play, and knew my intervention was at an end. I smiled at him.

"Well, there you are, old girl," I said. "Take it or leave it. It's up to you." (109–10)

Having thus given up on the pretensions of breeding as well as its economic possibilities, the narrator feels gratified in at least having given his "old girl" the satisfaction of sex. Unfortunately, neither he nor Tulip, nor Dusty for that matter, is prepared for that distinctly canine and unhuman moment of the "tie," which happens to dogs after successful intercourse, leaving them physically joined often for a half hour or more. The meeting between Tulip and Dusty is described as "charming" and "wonderfully pretty" until Tulip panics when she realizes Dusty is tied to her. She bolts, pulling the poor hapless stud around the garden: "Tulip gazed at me in horror and appeal. Heavens! I thought. This is love! These are the pleasures of sex!" (111). A while later, after the dogs have been calmed by the narrator and the tie has finally been broken, Dusty runs home "and was seen no more," while Tulip, who "seemed to think it was I who had saved her" (111), evinces "spectacular relief," "joy," and "gratitude": "It was more as though she had been freed from some dire situation of peril than from the embraces of love" (111).

Several things result from this incident. The first is the resulting litter of pups, which definitely proves that Tulip is not a "barren bitch"; their birthing and weaning are elaborately and tragicomically described by Ackerley in the ensuing chapter, "Fruits of Labor." After having succeeded in "placing" the puppies and reporting on the generally unhappy circumstances of their subsequent lives, at least to the extent of his knowledge, the narrator vows "never again" to repeat the terrible scenario of husband hunting, mating, and reproduction: "I had done my duty by Tulip; I had enabled her to have the full life it had always been my intention to give her; she had experienced sex and utilised her creative organs and maternal instincts; I need never have all that worry and trouble again" (134). Yet the story is not over, for the narrator seems to have completely conflated the sexuality of his female with the urge to have babies. It remains, in the final chapter, "The Turn of the Screw," for that premise to be undone and its holder disabused. In anticipation of this realization, a footnote appears on the same page of the quotation that was just cited. A certain Kenneth Walker is cited as saying, "There is no evidence that physical harm results from sexual continence. If any injury is inflicted by chastity, it is not on the body but on the mind," to which Ackerley adds, "Does this statement have any application to the lower animals?" (134).

The question of Tulip's sexual frustration becomes the explicit topic of the last chapter and an implicit commentary on the narrator's own frustrations in this area. In short, Ackerley describes the difficulties of living with Tulip's heat cycles after the decision has been made to have no more litters, no more breeding. The problem is not just that of keeping other dogs—potential suitors—out of Tulip's path but that of facing the intensity of her passion:

> Nature will not be cheated, fooled, bribed, fobbed off, shuffled out of the way. I still have to return in the evening and, dodge it as I may, I know what I shall find, a burning creature burning with desire. "Heat" is the apt word; one can feel against one's hand without touching her the feverous radiations from her womb. A fire has been kindled in it, and no substitute pleasure can distract, no palliative soothe, no exertion tire, no cooling stream slake, for long the all-consuming need of her body. She is enslaved. She is possessed. . . . How cruel a trick, I think, to concentrate, like a furnace, the whole of a creature's sexual desire into five or six weeks a year. Yet is she worse or better off than ourselves who seek gratification of it, without respite, over the great part of our lives? (141–43)

The rhetorical question that closes the passage draws Tulip's plight in line with that of the human "ourselves," who includes, at least, the narrator. Interestingly, the similarity drawn between human and animal is effected by the metaphor of "ardor," which connects the heat of passion in human beings with the animality of desire. In this case, however, "ardor" effectively anthropomorphizes a beast the nature of whose desire is as fever-pitched as that of any passionate human.

The anthropomorphic connection reveals a full-blown gay subtext in the description of Wimbledon Common, where the narrator takes Tulip on her morning walks even in the midst of her most intensive heats. A veritable bower of bliss or *locus amoenus* full of tress, birds, and small creatures, the birch woods are a "solitary place [that] belongs to us. It is our private garden, our temple, our ivory tower" (148). In the midst of this sacred grove lies a great birch tree whose anthropomorphic features readily lend themselves to interpretation: "Lord of the woods, like a giant buried upside down to the waist, his huge open legs, green at the thighs, tower sprawling into the air. The narrow track, hedged with high bracken, passes between them over his crutch. It is the heart of the woods, the sacred precinct, and with Tulip beside me I descend into it" (149). The tree's trampled "crutch" metaphorizes, of course, the theme of sexual frustration and denial of desire to the adjacent landscape, sacred to Tulip and the narrator precisely because she can be free to run around in this remote location of the park without fear (or hope!) of encountering a canine mate. The area is also known for its suicides, and it is saturated with the stories of those who "entered it to die," one by hanging himself in the dark, another by swallowing a poison after having "burrow[ed] into his green unwelcoming shroud [so deep] that it was many days before his body was found, his empty phial beside him" (153). Tulip's playground is the very locus of frustration and despair: "Who? Why? The failed, the frustrated lives pass on, leaving no trace. The place must be full of ghosts" (153). And at this point, in one of his most daring passages, Ackerley introduces the tragic story of Michael Holland, a young schoolboy who apparently committed suicide in a swampy part of Wimbledon Common after being hounded at school for his "effeminacy," use of perfume, avoidance of sports, and other "curious habits":[8]

> And young Holland, where did he die? Where is the swamp into which he drove his face? Lost, lost, the inconsiderable, anguished deed in the blind hurry of time. The perfect boy face downwards in a swamp.... The doctor who performed the autopsy remarked that the muscles and limbs were absolutely perfect, he had never seen a better developed boy in his life, nor, when he split open the skull, such deep grey matter. Ah, perfect but imperfect boy, brilliant at work, bored by games, traits of effeminacy were noticed in you, you were vain of your appearance and addicted to the use of scent. Everyone, it seemed, wished you different from what you were, so you came here at last and pushed your face into a swamp, and that was the end of you, perfect but imperfect boy. (153–54)

More than just another case of frustrated desire, Michael Holland incarnates the sense of deep alienation that comes from the social perception of one's otherness, of the punishment meted out to those who don't or won't "fit in" (to recall Johnny's ominous worldview). Such exclusion was, of course, keenly felt by Ackerley at a time when homosexuality was still officially a crime in Great Britain and certainly an object of potential censorship in printed literature, even as homosexual practices were common among the literate elite and the working classes. Ackerley knew this very well and in his long tenure as literary editor for

The Listener fought many a battle to open up freedom of expression for alternative sexualities.⁹ In fact, the original *London Times* article on Michael Holland in 1926 had inspired such militancy in Ackerley that his tribute to the boy in *My Dog Tulip* has much to do with an important settling of scores, not so much for this young boy as for all the victims of heterosexist exclusion and abuse: "It made a strong mark upon my young crusading homosexual mind and, one day, I thought, I will do something for young Holland, though possibly he was an odious youth. So you see he is, like all the rest, part of the true furniture of Wimbledon Common."¹⁰

The virtual equation between social exclusion and sexual frustration is the theme of the final chapter of *My Dog Tulip*, which begins by discussing the difficulties of getting Tulip in heat to a place where she can run freely, and in particular the power of bus conductors to allow or not allow man and dog to ride the bus. Tulip's explicit plight is most implicitly the narrator's, which is then made overt by the final reference to the death of Michael Holland and of a return to that crotchworn anthropomorphized birch tree:

> Out of their ragged green trousers the huge legs of the giant birch sprawl above my head. I pause for a moment upon his crutch and gaze fearfully upward. It looks no worse, the black mark and the thin trickle of blood, too high to reach, too high for my eyes at first to be sure, until I perceived the repulsive white fungi, like brackets, sprouting about it. He is sick, the great tree, he is doomed. It is a secret between us, but not for long will he escape the woodman's notice. They will cut off his legs, I think, as I pass between them prodding for glass. They will throw him down, the lord of the woods, they will throw him down. (154)

The allegorical lesson of the dying birch could not be clearer: sexual frustration and ostracism lead without redemption to disease, castration, and death. What an ironic commentary on the Walker quotation that textually closed chapter 5—as if chastity's "harm" could be restricted to the mind and not to the body! Ackerley's rhetorical question regarding the applicability of Walker's dictum to the "lower animals" is, in fact, answered by his reversal of the dichotomy between human and animal in favor of the animal and to the detriment of the human. Mindful of the equation between the beastly and the noble, we can conclude that what matters is not so much the lowliness of the animal as the lowest parts of an animal's anatomy that are revealed to us by the "upside-down" tree and, more generally, throughout this book (and Ackerley's subsequent writings), by the body of his bitch.

Tulip's bodily needs, whether defecation or heat cycle, are represented in Ackerley's texts not as lowly or disgusting but as in their own way valuable, beautiful, and noble. By taking a lesson from his dog (rather than through compulsion teaching her a lesson as "obedience" training) Ackerley can write such outrageous albeit oddly lyrical passages as those on Tulip's decision to urinate in some places—and indeed on some objects—and not others, or his eloquent description of her taking a shit—as well as his own downright pleasure in observing her do it:

> But apart from my interest in the results, it always pleases me to see her perform this physical act. She lowers herself carefully and gradually into a tripodal attitude with her hind legs splayed and her heels as far apart as she can get them so as not to soil her fur or her feet. Her long tail, usually carried aloft in a curve, unrolls and stretches rigidly out parallel with the ground, rather like one of those Christmas toys, called, I think, Giraffe's Tongues, which can be inflated into other people's faces and then recoil into one's own. Her ears lie back, her head cranes forward, and a mild, meditative look settles on her face. (33)

It is this unrepentant celebration of what Bakhtin calls the "material bodily stratum" that gives the book its humor as well as a certain scandalous edge, which doubles as an important plea for sexual toleration.

The meditation on Michael Holland and the "lord of the woods" is brought to a close by the dramatic return of Tulip onto the scene:

> There is a sudden scurry of noise, and Tulip flies across the ride on which I stand, her nose to the ground. Out of the tattered undergrowth on one side, into the tattered undergrowth on the other, she rushes; she has come, she has gone, silence claps down again, it is as though she had never been. Excepting that, caught upon the cinders of the ride in front of me curls and wavers in the frozen air the warm white fume of her breath. I watch it as it clings, writhes, wavers, slowly dissolves. She has been, she has gone, nothing now remains. Soon it will be over. Soon it will be too late. (155)

To the castrated birch corresponds the phallic bitch, scattering the spermatic "warm white fume of her breath" through "the frozen air." The book thus ends on a wistful note, "the turn of the screw," as, at least for the moment, the limited possibilities of bodily experience are lost, thwarted by the frustration the narrator feels he must impose on his bitch as a "responsible dog owner," thwarted by those social forces whose violence results in the fact that "the failed, the frustrated lives pass on, leaving no trace" (153).

On the other hand, there is a trace, certainly in the fact of Ackerley's text itself, whose inseminating qualities are perhaps best captured in that magical forest scene where Tulip's metaphorical semen "clings, writhes, slowly dissolves" between the legs of that effeminate male tree, itself a metaphor of the unhappy gays driven to their death there as well as the sexually frustrated, aging old trunk/twank of a narrator. And only in the final scene can the narrator imagine the truth about Tulip's sexual energy, which he has learned is not about her maternal needs, as he had simply and misogynistically assumed. Rather, Tulip is an immeasurably fecund element in Ackerley's own life, inspiring him to write again after a hiatus of nearly a quarter of a century (*Hindoo Holiday* was published in 1932, to be followed by *My Dog Tulip* only in 1956). If his writing about her is the trace we have not only of her but of him, that is also because she has inseminated him with the seed of inspiration, through a communion of mind that is the bond between man and beast, a communion not exclusive of a literal commingling of bodily liquids, as the narrator notes with glee at the end of "Liquids and Solids":

> There came a day, however, when we were walking in Wimbledon woods and she suddenly added my urine, which I had been obliged to void, to the other privileged objects of her social attention. How touched I was! How honoured I felt! "Oh Tulip! Thank you," I said.
> And now she always does it. No matter how preoccupied her mind may be with other things, such as rabbiting, she will always turn back, before following me, to the place where she saw me relieve myself—for nothing that I do escapes her—to sprinkle her own drops upon mine. So I feel that if ever there were differences between us they are washed out now. I feel a proper dog. (58)

Becoming a "proper dog" lets Ackerley perceive the world from a canine perspective, making him one of the greatest observers of dog behavior, anticipating scientific discoveries about the ritual and socially communicative aspects of excremental markings, for example, which he describes in protoscientific terms as a form of writing, "endorsing . . . things with her signature, much as we underline a book we are reading" (48).

The discovery of nobility and "literacy" in the reputedly low life of dogs is celebrated in class terms as well, on a first level, throughout the book, in the general antipathy shown toward upper-class owners and their high-bred pooches: "the smarter [the dog's] postal address the fainter his hopes" of finding a mate (157). "In working-class areas, where greater laxity and muddlement prevail, his chances of self-help are somewhat better" (157), we are told, but even there disgust, erotophobia, and the concomitant fear of animals suggest that "the fact that one seldom sees dogs copulating in the streets might seem circumstantial evidence of the rarity of the event" (157). On a second level, Tulip's sexual preferences decidedly lie on the nonpedigreed mongrel side, something Ackerley, flying in the face of the conventional practice of breeding only purebred to purebred, is led to view in a positive light:

> But in all my questionings about the sexual lives of dogs, I have never met anyone who deliberately threw, as I did, a pedigree bitch to a mongrel though I have met a few pedigree bitches who managed to throw themselves to mongrels and got families thereby. The trial-and-error stories I hear, from which after one failure, owners draw the perhaps convenient conclusion that since bitch refused dog or dog refused bitch, dog or bitch does not really like sex at all, are always intra-breed matches. The inference may be true; but I often wonder nevertheless whether the result would have been the same if the animals had been allowed to choose for themselves. A woman biologist, when told that Tulip had appeared to prefer a mongrel sire, remarked: "Shows her good sense." (161)

Only recently, in the light of the extraordinary failure of sanctioned breeding and the resultant destruction of the most popular dog breeds by line-breeding and inbreeding, which only intensify genetic defects from generation to generation rather than eliminating them, as was mistakenly assumed, has some serious criticism of the kennel establishment finally been made. Most surprisingly, Ackerley closes his appendix by reciting a story of a working-class dog owner who wanted sex for his frustrated dog, hoping a bitch "might cool his ardour off" (164), but reacted with unbelievable indignation when the narrator suggests he let the dog loose with a mongrel bitch living in the same street. The irony, of course, is that of a class prejudice projected by a working-class dog owner onto his purebred dog, as if to condone the very concept of class hierarchy based in a mere hereditary privilege.

Finally, Tulip's taste in dogs ironically mirrors the narrator's own hankering after working-class youth. But this similarity too suggests another solution to their common frustration, one that would involve an implicit or explicit satisfaction of each other's needs. Such a solution, whether it be ever so mildly expressed in the direction of bestial love, remains a much greater taboo even than homosexuality. Yet Ackerley leaves enough clues to draw some conclusions about the satisfaction of sexual need in an otherwise forbidding and repressive environment. And the dogs themselves provide the answer, as could not escape the gaze of this acutely attentive observer: "Knowing nothing, in spite of constant efforts to inform them, of the Expulsion from Eden, dogs remain lamentably innocent and uninhibited in their emotions; worse, they are all too liable to confuse sex and pleasure and, having no outlet for the former, to address the whole boiling to their beloved owners. Tulip herself, when I offer her some delicious prospect such as an unexpected walk, will often try to rape me as we go down in the lift, a demonstration of gratitude I should regard myself as churlish to rebuff. But normally such behaviour is ill-received and checked" (163). Once again the narrator makes a discovery by taking a passive or feminine role: here it is the form of the affection displayed by Tulip's "raping" him in gratitude for a walk, just as earlier it was her marking his urine, and, in the autobiographical novel, her substitutive play of desire, which defines, originates, and perpetuates the bond between human and animal. Reciprocal attention, then, is what Tulip requests from him most urgently in the lengthy description of her all-consuming "heat" in the "Turn of the Screw" chapter.

Nor are such requests limited to her human master: "This independent, unapproachable, dignified and single-hearted creature, my devoted bitch, becomes the meekest of beggars. Anyone will do who will supply her with a crumb of physical comfort" (142). Ironically, "people are often flattered when animals seem to select them for affection," but this is simply because "human beings are extraordinarily ignorant about dogs. These amused and flattered people do not notice the coiling tail; if they noticed it they would not know what it meant; if they knew what it meant they would probably be less flattered and amused" (142). Such interspecies promiscuity is pleasing and "amusing" to all, provided its "meaning" is barred from cognition (i.e., repressed): "They stroke her. If they stroke her head, that is not what she wants; she will shift herself further round to present them with her rump" (142). When the sexual meaning of such affectionate behavior is revealed, however, human erotophobia knows no bounds: "'Send her to kennels. That's what we always do.' 'Haven't you a spare room to shut her up in?' 'Have her altered.' And then the voice I most fear and detest: 'Kick her out of the road, the dirty bitch!'" (145).

Such responses are out of the question for a narrator who, as we have seen, is on many levels identified with his dog and cannot abide what he clearly sees as the signs of her frustrated sexual desire without responding with heartfelt sympathy, given his own identical state of mind. The only question is who has it worse: "How cruel a trick, I think, to concentrate, like a furnace, the whole of a creature's sexual desire into five or six weeks a year. Yet is she worse or better off than ourselves who seek gratification of it, without respite, over the greater part of our lives?" (143).

Despite his best efforts, and despite the misadventures he previously described, in trying to breed her and raise her pups, he cannot resist Tulip's demands, potent concentrate as they are of his own pent-up urges:

> "Help me," she says, gazing at me with her confident animal eyes; but I no longer wish to help her, I wish to frustrate her, I wish her to have everything in the world she wants, except the thing she needs. She presses up against me. I put down my hand and stroke her, her soft ears, her pretty head, her backbone, her coiling tail. The tail is sign enough of her physical torment. So rigid is it that a small effort is required to disengage it from the flank to which it clings. When I draw it though my hand it recoils upon her body like a steel spring, and whips, as though endued with a life of its own, from side to side. (143)

As happens with the public bystanders whose affectionate "pets" Tulip elicits, the narrator finds his hand drawn steadily down from head to "coiling tail," the latter having "a life of its own" whose phallic significance leaves us no room for doubt: "So rigid is it that a small effort is required to disengage it from the flank to which it clings" (143).

The same scene is repeated a page later, this time in a visual register:

> "Help me," she says, pressing against me, staring up into my face, bringing me her trouble. I cannot bear it. With a rough word I send her from me. She goes, dejected, rebuffed (dogs are expert at inflicting remorse), and sits on the bed at the other side of the room facing me. Unendurable the hopeful gaze watching for signs of relentment, the sorry sighs she heaves. A smile would bring her over, even a look. I avert my face. But she cannot rest. Nature will not let her rest. Soon she has slid off the bed, and by a halting, circuitous route, reached me again to replace herself in my line of vision. The tall ears are erect now, the head drawn back, the gaze level. I meet it, in spite of myself. We stare into each other's eyes. The look in hers disconcerts me, it contains too much, much more than a beast may give, something too clear and too near, too entire, too dignified and direct, a steadier look than my own. I avert my face. (143–44)

In Ackerley's revision here of the Petrarchan erotic narrative, the female other penetrates the passive, male viewer with her "disconcerting" gaze, turning him not into the *subject* of a desire whose intensity (and poetic inspiration) is in function of a lack but rather into the privileged *object* of a desire whose denial is inevitably overcome by a laying on of hands, this time not from the narrator but from Tulip herself:

> I avert my face. Raising a paw she bangs me on the knee.
> "No, Tulip."
> But delicately finding room for her fore-feet on the seat of my chair, she rises up towards me and sets her cheek to mine. (144)

The feminized narrator can only further the bitch's ardor by his "no," and she assumes, like the insistent male seducer of tradition, that "no" does not *mean* "no" but rather "yes," a canine assertion of overt sexual meaning legitimized by the human's looking away from the staring animal in what the dog, as every dog psychologist or trainer knows, will immediately interpret as a sign of submission and surrender, and here, the formal recognition of the bitch's dominance. Still, unwittingly encouraging the dog by his very efforts to deny her, the narrator decides to retire for the evening, only to have his horny pet follow him straight into bed:

> I go to bed early to end the dismal day, but she is instantly beside me, sitting upright against my pillow, her back turned, shifting, licking, panting, shifting, peering at my face, pulling at my arm. Sweet creature, what am I doing to you? I stretch out my hand in the gloom and stroke the small nipples which, I have decided, shall never again fulfill their natural purpose. Panting she slackly sits while my hand caresses her, her ears flattened, her head drooped, gazing with vacant eyes into the night beyond the windows. Gradually she relaxes, subsides. Gradually, my hand upon her, she sleeps. (144–45)

Beyond the question of who seduces whom in this sequence of events, the "meaning" of the human hand stroking canine nipples et al. is made clear in a passage from *We Think the World of You*, late in the story when Johnny comes to visit Evie at Frank's home. Johnny, who is still the recipient of great affection from the dog as he was her original owner, knows exactly how to reciprocate this affection, and he shows Frank how it's done:

> . . . when she had done making love to him he would make love to her. He knew—it was what he was good at—exactly where and how to touch her, and as soon as his hand descended she would roll over on her side and open her legs, and his strong yet gentle fingers would move over her stomach, manipulating her nipples and her neat, pretty genital, shaped like a daffodil [or tulip?], in the way she enjoyed, while he whispered little affectionate obscenities into her ears. "Is this it, gal?? Is that what you like?" he would say, and she would sigh and swoon away beneath him. (164–65)

Even though this passage was extensively revised and re-edited before publication, an even more explicit version of the episode can be found in Ackerley's diary entry of November 1, 1948, when the author describes an unexpected visit by Freddie that also unexpectedly leads to *everyone's* satisfaction:

> Queenie is tremendously fond of him, I don't quite know why, unless it is that she has still some childish memory of him or senses his fondness for her, and after eating we went into my bedroom, where Queenie began to make a fuss of him and he of her. He began to tickle her tits and the base of her little vulva, saying 'Is that what you like? Is this what you like?' Queenie reacted most touchingly and extraordinarily, exactly as if she were human. She took it mostly sitting up, facing away from him towards—at—me, sometime looking round and down when he left her tits for her cunt. Her ears were back, her eyes simply liquid, welling with softness, happiness and pleasure. (36–37)

Not only is the sexual meaning of the reciprocal affection more evident, but the beast's responsiveness narrows the difference between the species, causing her to be "exactly as if she were human" and later "extremely beautiful, and most human" (37). Watching this, the diarist addresses not the human lover but the beastly one, referring to his human lover in the third person and underscoring the workings of a ménage à trois: "I said, 'Oh Queenie, isn't he nice. He gives one such pleasure. Now it's your turn. Next it will be mine'" (37). Freddie too addresses Queenie directly ("Is this it, gal? Is this what you like? Is this it, Queen? Do you like this?" [37]), before he addresses or rather instructs his human partner with a bit of carnal knowledge that is presented as the privileged information of a heterosexual man. He thereby underscores the difference between the human lovers at the same time that the difference with the canine one is effaced: "Freddie smiled and went on tickling and whispering to her, caressing and tickling her tits with his large gentle fingers with their grubby nails. 'This is where women like it, I know,' he said, moving his finger to the base of her cunt. And old Queenie sat there, quite united with us, putting out something human and intelligible though speechless thro' her eyes, an immense and humble happiness" (37). This intimate depiction of interspecies and intergender lovemaking then makes the subsequent intraspecies and intragender sex narratively redundant to the extent that the act itself involves the same kind of digital manipulation.

If we recall Ackerley's own description and analysis of his sexual predilections in *My Father and Myself*, published posthumously but completed in manuscript before his death, the full import of the "sexual" activity described above becomes clear. For although Ackerley's introspective last work explores the roots and meaning of his own homosexuality, the actual range of the sexual practices he embraced seems rather narrow, excluding as it does both oral and anal penetration. Here is what he writes of fellatio: "It is a form of pleasure I myself have seldom enjoyed, passively or actively, preferring the kiss upon the lips, nor have I ever been good at it. Some technical skill seems required and a retraction of the teeth which, perhaps because mine are too large or unsuitably arranged, seem always to get in the way. Squeamishness with comparative strangers over dirt or even disease disturbs me . . . and to be practically choked for ten minutes or so after one's own orgasm has passed is something I have never enjoyed."[11] Moreover, his four-year affair with the sailor Albert, perhaps Ackerley's closest realization of the Ideal Friend, is said to have fallen apart because of an ill-fated attempt at oral sex (129–30). As for sodomy, Ackerley claimed to be "quite impenetrable" but suffered a bout of gonorrhea when he yielded to a young grenadier, who "begged so hard to be allowed at any rate to try" (140). Finally, Ackerley complains throughout of his insuperable repulsion by effeminacy in men, lisps, bad breath, and body odors (in particular from damp feet), as well as an anxiety about his own sexual incontinence and later impotence. All of this has led to some confusion about what Ackerley's sexuality consisted of, which seems ironic for such a scandalous confessional narrative as *My Father and Myself*. As W.H. Auden remarked, "Frank as he is, Mr. Ackerley is never quite explicit about what he *really* preferred to do in bed."[12]

Actually, the answer lies first of all in his sexual incontinence, of which, as he elaborates in the appendix to *My Father and Myself*, he was "deeply ashamed" (210). There he describes his state of arousal as being such that "a kiss, then, the mere pressure of an embrace, if I got as far as that, was enough to finish me off—and provide a new shame, that the stain, seeping through my trousers, might be seen" (210). While alluding to an etiology of anxiety and guilt, Ackerley also cites early schoolboy experiences involving genital touching ("sitting beside Jude in class and letting him guide my hand through the opened seam of his trouser pocket" [210]) as contributing to this "affliction," which "put an end to my own pleasure before it had begun and, with the expiry of my desire, which was never soon renewed, my interest in the situation, even in the person, causing me to behave inconsiderately to him" (210). It seems clear that such a propensity would make more ambitious sexual activity dispensable. When he describes his affair with Albert before the fatal attempt at oral sex, the "pleasures" he enumerates remain "fairly simple, kisses, caresses, manipulations, intercrural massage; he got his own satisfaction quite soon, though not as soon as I" (128). And given what we've already seen, such was certainly the gist of his sexual encounters with Freddie.

But, then, what about Queenie? Any rubbing, touching, or digital manipulation of her would seem virtually indistinguishable from, if not a clear continuation of, Ackerley's described sexual conduct. The final two pages of *My Father and Myself*, in fact, finally address this question, though in a way that seems designed to throw a less than attentive reader far off scent. Queenie makes her appearance at the end of this self-analytical exercise as the solution to Ackerley's unhappy love life. The roots of this life are explored through his poignant investigation into a family history full of secrets and duplicity: "It is for me, the interesting part of this personal history that peace and contentment reached me in the shape of an animal, an Alsatian bitch" (216). As he recalls his first work of literature, Ackerley nevertheless invites the reader to view that solution as unconsciously foreseen by one of his characters: "Is it, I wonder, of any value as a clue to my psychology to recall that in my play *The Prisoners of War* the hero, Captain Conrad (myself of course), unable to build on human relations, takes to a plant? He tells some story of another imprisoned officer who fell in love with a pet rabbit and read short stories to it out of a magazine. 'Plants or rabbits,' he says, 'it's the same thing'" (216). Conrad's remark, of course, which universally embraces its love objects to include virtually all living things, and totally overturns the progressive exclusivity that propels the history of Ackerley's desire, where finally the only acceptable object of desire remotely capable of meeting his criteria for the Greek ideal friend is to be found in young London guardsmen who are devoid of either effeminacy or body odors and are willing to spend time with an old "twank" for a few extra pounds sterling. This libidinal blind alley is revealed to be its own psychological impasse when Ackerley discovers that his father may have behaved similarly when he served in the Guards a generation earlier. And, as we recall, the last of this series of young guardsmen was the notorious Freddie, whose jail time brought Queenie directly into Ackerley's life. But if the disastrous relation with Freddie represents perhaps the final psychical chapter in a son's failure to secure the love of his father, Alfred, the entrance of Queenie into his life can hardly be said to be a simple transfer of libido from a highly particular love object (the father) to just anything at all ("Plants or rabbits, it's the same thing"). This is particularly so if we remember the role of the dog's own agency in seducing Ackerley, an agency Ackerley both reaffirms and then denies in the following passage: "This bitch of mine entered my life in the middle 'forties and entirely transformed it. I have already described her in two books; it is necessary to say here that I don't believe there was anything special about her, except that she was rather a beauty. In this context it is not she herself but her effect upon me that I find interesting. She offered me what I had never found in my sexual life, constant, single-hearted, incorruptible, uncritical devotion, which it is in the nature of dogs to offer. She placed herself entirely under my control" (216–17). Of course, it is precisely Queenie's uncontrollability yet demonstrable loyalty and affection that are both the theme of the love affair between man and bitch *and* the very source of Ackerley's attachment to her. We need only remember the narrator's first walk with Evie in *We Think the World of You,* where her unruly and dangerously headstrong behavior *on* leash is contrasted with her fidelity *off* leash, or the nobility found precisely in her *beastliness.* It is the status of *her* desire that will prevail, to what seems to be the extinction of his own:

> From the moment she established herself in my heart and home, my obsession with sex fell wholly away from me. The pubs I had spent so much of my time in were never revisited, my single desire was to get back to her, to her waiting love and unstaling welcome. . . . I never prowled the London streets again, nor had the slightest inclination to do so. On the contrary, whenever I thought of it, I was positively thankful to be rid of it all, the anxieties, the frustrations, the wastage of time and spirit. It was as though I had never wanted sex at all, and that this extraordinary long journey of mine which had seemed a pursuit of it had really been an attempt to escape from it. I was just under fifty when this animal came into my hands, and the fifteen years she lived with me were the happiest of my life. (217)

Obviously, this sudden change in Ackerley's way of life could not fail to raise questions of the sort with which I myself began this chapter, questions of the sort Ackerley now puts in the mouth of "one of [his] friends," who, "puzzled by the sudden change in my ways, asked me whether I had sexual intercourse with her" (217). We need to understand the term *sexual intercourse* in the most traditional and restrictive way if we are to read Ackerley's answer: "It may be counted as something on the profit side of my life that I could now receive such a question intelligently. I said no" (217). But this "intelligent answer" is then followed by a different one, by the "truth": "In truth, her love and beauty when I kissed her, as I often did, sometimes stirred me physically" (217). This truth, which *is* the truth of desire, speaks of something utterly other than what is evoked by the clinical and conjugal terminology of sexual "intercourse." Physical arousal, as the final pages of *My Father and Myself* have shown, is almost coterminous with its satisfaction, or the shame of what Ackerley calls his incontinence. Yet what one might be inclined to call the autotelic or self-satisfying quality of erotic passion in Ackerley does not begin to prepare us for the startling non sequitur that closes the sentence: "In truth, her love and beauty when I kissed her, as I often did, sometimes stirred me physically; but although I had to cope with her own sexual life and the frustrations I imposed upon it for some years, the thought of attempting to console her myself, even with my finger, never seriously entered my head" (218). Grammatically (and the effect is powerful in the case of so consummate a stylist as J.R. Ackerley), what should follow the admission of "physical" arousal is that, although Queenie too was also in her way aroused, the author did not follow through on *his* own desire *for her*. Instead, we are told that, despite his and her desires for each other, he never ever thought of trying to assuage *her* desire. Of course, if, as we have learned, his desire is virtually self-satisfying, requiring a mere touch as an orgasmic trigger, then the only question will indeed be the fate of her desire. And in the following lines, the assertion that he never attempted even to "console" her is flatly contradicted as Ackerley explicitly describes what he nonetheless "did for her":

> What little I did for her in her burning heats—slightly more than I admitted in *My Dog Tulip*—worried me in my ignorance of animal psychology, in case, by gratifying her clear desires, which were all addressed to me, I might excite and upset her more than she was already excited and upset. The most I ever did for her was to press my hand against the hot swollen vulva she was always pushing at me at these times, taking her liquids upon my palm. This small easement was, of course, nearer the thing she wanted than to have her back, tail and nipples stroked. (218)

What he now "admits" to doing for her is really no more and no less than what he himself craved from his human lovers: "Yet looking at her sometimes I used to think that the Ideal Friend, whom I no longer wanted, perhaps never had wanted, should have been an animal-man, the mind of my bitch, for instance, in the body of my sailor, the perfect human male body always at one's service through the devotion of a faithful and uncritical beast" (218).

The issue in all this is not whether Ackerley's heavy petting qualifies as "sex." And on this key question, it is to psychoanalysis's credit to have expanded the definition of the sexual far beyond the heteronormative rule of penile-vaginal penetration to include the virtual totality of human behavior beyond the strict necessities of self-preservation.[13] Rather, what Ackerley's texts bring to the fore is the clearly sexual character of the relation between humans and pets, not so much in terms of the explicit bestiality that so concerns Midas Dekkers in his study on humans and pets *(Dearest Pet),* but rather in terms of the eroticism at work in all *intersubjective* relations (whether between human beings of the same or different genders or between beings of the same or different species). The human impulse to interact physically and emotionally with animals, to gaze at them, talk to them, stroke them, can scarcely be differentiated from the need to interact similarly with other human beings.

Indeed, Ackerley's point would seem to be that *only* humans remain unaware of this generalized eroticism. The interchangeability of the characters along the axis of desire in *We Think the World of You* is, we have seen, a veritable object lesson in this regard, as, in another vein, are the self-contradictory human attitudes to canine sexuality in *My Dog Tulip*. Friendly "pets" are always welcome so long as the potentially sexual nature of the touching is denied, ignored, or repressed. I say "potentially sexual" again to underscore the notion that the beast does not represent the sharp intrusion of the sexual into some presumably nonsexual human existence but rather that the beast, at least as Ackerley conceives of its being, is what makes the difference between the sexual and the nonsexual indistinguishable. It is the beastliness of the beast, in other words, that becomes the term for the realm of the repressed that classic Freudianism has polemically demarcated as sexuality. For, in Ackerley's view, what makes the beast a beast (and *a fortiori* what makes for the beauty of the beast) is not just the satisfaction of self-preservative needs but the unrestrained display of behavior that freely, even shockingly, exceeds self-preservation and sates what traditional Western discourse has for much too long and too readily termed the "animal instincts." The attribution of such behavior to various sectors of the human race itself in order to dehumanize them by recalling their animality, which is in us all, is of course deeply implicated in the history of ethnocentrism, racism, sexism, classism, and other ideologies of privilege.[14] And apart from his own obvious and inevitable entrapment in such discourses, Ackerley invites us to consider the opposite, namely that it is the human rejection of the beast that constitutes humanity's inhumanity.

Two examples clarify this paradox in appearance only. The first is to be found in the first chapter of *My Dog Tulip* when the narrator contrasts Tulip's unsociable and uncontrollable behavior on visits to the veterinarian with that of another dog, a model pet Spaniel "who was being treated as we arrived":

> This creature was visible to us, like some callous admonishment, before ever we reached the door, for the window of the surgery looked out upon a yard through which we had to pass, and the Spaniel was all too plainly seen within.
> He was standing quietly on a table with a thermometer sticking out of his bottom, like a cigarette. And this humiliating spectacle was rendered all the more crushing by the fact that there was no one else there. Absolutely motionless, and with an air of deep absorption, the dog was standing upon the table in an empty room with a thermometer in his bottom, almost as though he had put it there himself.
> 'Oh, Tulip!' I groaned. 'If only you were like that!' (15)

Nothing, of course, could be further from Ackerley's own sense of eros without penetration than this image of a clinically sodomized animal. Indeed, despite the narrator's initial wish that Tulip were "only like that," he later comes to fully recognize the value of his bitch's own contrasting beastliness as an authentic case of (nonhuman, i.e., fully "other") otherness that cannot be eradicated or overcome, even by the ensuing brutality used by the veterinarian ("this odious little man" [16]) to subdue her for treatment. Only later, after having successfully visited a female veterinarian evincing a calm and matter-of-fact approach does he once again worry, not this time about his dog's undisciplined behavior but about an excessive obedience that would turn her from being a "tigress" into "must I face it?—an ordinary dog": "Was it not even possible that, in course of time, under these civilising processes, she would become so tame, so characterless, so commonplace, that she might one day be found standing in a surgery alone with a thermometer in her bottom?" (30). Tulip, of course, "never let[s him] down" (30) and retains her beastliness in her heats and otherwise, never allowing herself to submit to a cold humanity that would penetrate her with an instrument designed to calculate body temperature. Her beastliness, as we have seen here so often, remains the very sign of her beauty and nobility.

A second and final example can be found in a very late piece by Ackerley, a short article written for *Orient/West Magazine* in 1964: the overtly provocative and scandalous "I Am a Beast." Ackerley's embraces a "beastly" perspective, not merely to defend the beastliness of beasts, but also to take an ethically necessary and critical view of humankind. This literally inhuman point of view is asserted not only in the title but also in the text's outrageous opening line: "I dislike children." Rather than being the familiar representation of human innocence and potential for good, children, in Ackerley's view, become incomprehensibly other to the extent that they represent the human potential for harm, in particular toward other creatures on the planet: "I dislike children. They seem incomprehensible, like inebriates. They inhabit a world of their own which I cannot enter, and the scenery and props of which I look in soon bore me, it is so restless, senseless, and noisy. Moreover, they go on being children for such an awfully long time. Will they *never* grow up? Then they grow up and become adults, and that is worse than ever. But then you see, I am a beast."[15] As is so typical of Ackerley's prose works, the "I" that speaks here is partially autobiographical, partially ventriloquized. In this case, it is the voice of what is on the brink of extinction and to which "man" has long stopped listening, the voice of the beast. The complete extent of the human domination of the globe now means that animals are no longer safe from human beings, save perhaps ironically in zoos (of which "of course there are zoos and zoos" [68]). Everywhere, "animals are rapidly being squeezed as man, with his ever-increasing need for space and food, encroaches upon their final habitats . . . and where the interests of man conflict with the interests of animals, the latter stand no chance at all" (67–68). Zoos, awful as they usually are, exist then "not to protect people from the animals, which is the human fancy, but to protect the animals from people. Fences they must have; where there are no fences they are doomed; even behind bars they are not safe" (71). This is where the beastly dislike of children comes in, as Ackerley recounts an unfortunate incident at a British zoo:

> A few years ago some small boys, out of control of their supervisor, clambered onto the top of a cage in Whipsnade Park in which the lions had been temporarily segregated while their paddock was being cleaned. Taunting and provoking the lions they poked at them with sticks until one sprang up and seized the arm of his tormentor. He let go only when the supervisor arrived and struck him with an iron bar. Bulletins about the child's health, as he lay in hospital between life and death, were issued daily in the press. Until he died, some days later, he was front-page news. No bulletins were issued about the health of the lion, who had been struck on the head with an iron bar, and no one inquired after him. I myself wrote a letter of inquiry for publication, but I did not send it . . . and in the sacred hush that enveloped this child's sick-bed I was as scared as I would be to remain seated while

the National Anthem is being played. Animals don't matter, only people matter. (71–72)

Again, any attempt on the part of animals to resist human intervention and penetration is met with swift and uncompromising force. Animals have no court of appeals and can allege no mitigating circumstances. Earlier in the essay, Ackerley goes even further, questioning the nature of human kindness to animals: "I often wonder whether kindness to animals, wherever it may be claimed to exist, would be so described by the animals themselves, if they could speak. Do wild birds enjoy to be in cages however plentiful their food supply? And although it may be convenient . . . to take dogs for a run by pulling them along a leash behind a bicycle, the dogs, whose great pleasure in life is olfactory, would not describe this as a kindness" (68). As for those who wish to speak out on behalf of beasts, to explain their most beastly behavior, they risk the extreme censure of those who question the rituals of civic pride and patriotism.

What, then, puts Ackerley in a position to be able to speak up as an animal advocate in this instance? He explains how it is that he "became a beast" by recounting yet a final time the story of what he is now happy to call his "involvement" with Queenie:

> Then I became involved with an animal, an Alsatian bitch. She lived with me for fifteen years, and the constant fixture of her gaze upon my face gained my reciprocal attention. When she was young I attempted to instruct her in the ways of the human world; I was able to teach her practically nothing. Whatever she thought it advisable to know she picked up for herself; all other exhortations and commands she resisted. Perhaps I could have forced her to obey me had I wished, but I did not wish; obedience and character cannot both be had and I was interested in the free development of her character. She said she knew better than I and, as time passed, I respected and yielded to her opinions more and more. . . . Thus was *she* able to instruct *me*. (69; emphasis in original)

Here, finally, Ackerley acknowledges that what he learned from Queenie was not what he taught or might have trained her to do but what she taught him, training him in the way of the beasts, a "humbling knowledge" that revealed to him not only "that her character was infinitely sweeter than [his] own" but also that "this new country which opened up for me in the beam of her eye . . . was not new, I belonged to it, it was my original home" (69). Thus through Queenie's guidance Ackerley was finally able "in her presence" to recognize and proclaim out loud that "I am a beast." The wisdom imparted by animals is that of the beastliness human beings deny in themselves, thereby wreaking havoc far greater than any beast: "I am a beast, but I would not have it thought that I hate people. Animals do not have hatred, only people have hatred. Are there any of my wild guises in which I have not readily responded to overtures of human friendship? It was man who disdained our relationship, invented for himself the terrible word 'human,' and dubbed me with such cruel names as 'game' and 'pest.' And the higher he soars above me in his arrogance and power the lonelier he becomes" (72). Framed by Ackerley's polemic in defense of animal protection and the lessons of his involvement with Queenie is the essay's centerpiece, a description of his encounter with a caged tigress at a zoo in Matsushima, Japan. (Let us remember, of course, that in praising her most beastly unruliness, Ackerley hoped that Tulip/Queenie would remain more of a "tigress" than a civilized pooch like the Spaniel at the veterinarian's office.) Caught in a knowing exchange of gazes with the tigress, Ackerley describes her crouching down in expectation of a game: "I knew that she recognized me and I knew what she was doing, my bitch had explained all that, it was a game, a 'Chase me' game, she had played with me and other dogs countless times in her youth. . . . She was asking to be chased" (70). Sadly, the movement required to play out the game is prevented by the close dimensions of the tigress's cage. When he approaches her, she does not move; instead, "her watching eyes glazed over to a dim, dull look," and then "she got slowly up and resumed her restless prowling to and fro, rubbing her cheeks against the wire netting as she went" (70):

> Whenever she turned at the limit of these short, dismal journeyings, her eyes came round to meet mine. Was this all that remained to her of life, I wondered, excepting food? Was there anyone she loved and looked forward to seeing, like the panther in Balzac's story? Her keeper, for instance? Was he affectionate to her? Did he tickle her ears and the nipples on that soft pale stomach she had shown me? It would be some small compensation for the poverty and tedium of her life. Or was her meat just cast at her by a nervous hand? The door of her den was shut. (70)

Being himself a "beast," the narrator finds himself powerfully and indeed erotically connected to the tigress, through the quasi-Petrarchan communion of the eyes, through the reference to Balzac's "Une Passion dans le désert," and through the reminiscence of his own tactile play with Queenie.

A strong "sensation of melancholy" comes into the picture here. The context of zoological entrapment, humiliation, and abuse bars any further development of Ackerley's fantasy. The tigress is "on exhibition," the door to her den closed to prevent any retreat or escape from "the boredom of being gazed at." Furthermore, the double injustice of this forced exhibition and the loss of the human ability to communicate with the beasts, even in the simplest of ways, frames the human construction of the beast whose "nature" the captured beast in turn must display to content the human spectator who pays to see it: "And just to be on view, even that would not suffice. Suppose that, tired out by her aimless prowlings, she fell asleep on the floor of the cage. That would not do either. It would hardly be our money's worth. Tigers must behave in their tiger character, that fierce aggressive character invented for them by the big game hunter to enable him to boast of his valor in shooting them. A sleeping tigress would be a disappointment to the children" (70). Ackerley returns to his guiding polemic, recounting horrific stories of zoo animals taunted, provoked, and physically harmed by spectators eager to see them as they are imagined to be. This sequence builds up, of course, to the terrible event of the boy killed by the lion in the British zoo. Along the way, Ackerley describes the plight of a sea lion in Marseilles: "It was a pity that a pebble had struck her in the eye, which was suppurating, but then she should have been performing for us in the water instead of lying on a rock like a sack, having a doze. What is the good of animals if they don't perform? It is what the children enjoy. Laziness or headaches cannot be permitted. Animals are not allowed headaches, only people get headaches" (71). The only hopeful note is struck by his description of the tigress, Kaseh, and her cubs at the special Whipsnade zoological garden in Bedfordshire: "A high metal fence guarded her from human interference; she seems, in fact, quite unaware of the spectators above her, and was therefore able to live in her true tiger character which, far from being aggressive, is of a retiring disposition, especially where man is concerned" (71). Here, at last, albeit in restricted conditions, the beast can still be itself, still be a beast: "I am in man's way, my days are numbered I know, and I would sooner end them, like Kaseh, fed and protected than be left without a fence to larger freedom and the mercy of men" (72).

Published less than three years after Queenie's death, "I Am a Beast" anticipates the modern animal rights movement at the same time that it is deeply indebted to the theriophilic humanism of the Renaissance, which praises the superiority of the beasts over man.[16] "I Am a Beast" is less a melancholic piece than a true work of mourning in the technical Freudian sense: that is, less a narcissistic imputation of lack than a grieving working-through of loss by the ritualized decathexis of affect that takes place in the remembrance of a lost love. Thus, as Ackerley recalls his involvement with Queenie, the transfer of libido back onto his ego leads, not to a narcissistic investment in the self, but rather to the recognition that what he most loved in her—her beastly nobility or noble beastliness—is also what lies most within him. As such, Queenie becomes emotionally and even chronologically identical with the tigress of Matsushima: "I glanced back. The tigress was standing motionless, her gaze fixed upon me. The sensation of melancholy I had been acquiring choked me. When she saw me returning to her she crouched again. 'Goodbye, lovely lady,' I said. 'I wish I had not seen you and I shall never see you more.' That was three years ago and she has paced up and down my heart as, if she is still alive, I suppose she has paced up and down her cage ever since" (71).

Afterword

The very notion implied in the concept and practice of polymorphism, as envisioned in this book, is that living creatures cannot be reduced to a single model or body. The model of a polymorphous domesticity evoked here is both dynamic and fluid in structure. In it, a plurality of bodies challenge the anthropocentric tendency to view the human subject as central to itself (even though some of the readings point to a dystopian polymorphous space). Edith Wharton, Djuna Barnes, and Colette, three modern "Dianas," both revise and embody her myth and thus open up a role for animals to play in their particular reconfigurations of domestic space. The power of this myth is seen, for example, in how all three imaginatively redraw the space of home life so that the patriarchal household headed by a dominating *pater familias* becomes just one among many possibilities. In the non-normative domestic spaces that they depict, living creatures, multivalent sexualities, and polymorphous impulses together exclude any reduction of their lives into a single unit. J.R. Ackerley, the only male author in this book, testifies to how such a polymorphous space impedes any reductive narrative about gender and/or sexuality. Literary portrayals of polymorphous domestic relations between different beings, whether humans of the same or different sex, or nonhuman creatures, raise significant questions about the potentials inherent in these relations and challenge our received understandings of what it is to be human or animal. They reconceptualize domestic space as a zoomorphic world, one in which humans and animals live side by side, enjoying each other's company. Such a model disassembles anthropocentric and normative structures and inscribes animals as worthy of moral consideration. In this polymorphous world, bodies interact and play in a dynamic exchange of species, acting upon and being acted upon, transforming the relation of human to animal and animal to human by reshaping bodies through modes of cohabitation where animals are prominently figured. That this space is utopic also goes without saying, for within any domestic setting work is involved, especially for the *Homo sapiens* occupying and managing a domestic space. At the same time, this refigured world, managed by humans, ought to be understood as a place where humans who share their space with other species manage it *not* because they claim a superiority mandated by traditional paradigms of human supremacy over nature but simply because management happens to be one of many human skills. What does underlie this alternate notion of management is the recognition of a shared finitude: one of vulnerability and the mutual capacity to feel pain, to suffer and die, but also to feel joy.

In attempting to describe the polymorphous world discussed in this book, I turn to my own home, shared with several dogs, a cat, and horses. Its domestic life revolves around different creatures whose nonverbal communication is a language, indeed languages, "spoken" by and through eyes, gestures, and sounds. The home space is like the stage for dancers, where affect is freely expressed as moving bodies shapeshift while crossing boundaries of communication between human and nonhuman. It is a domesticated wild zone, a term that may sound oxymoronic but captures the sense of fluid boundaries. It is "domestic" in the sense that all the animals who interact with each other, myself among them, are domesticated creatures: whether my companions live in the house or in the barn, they live *with* and *beside* me, as well as with their own set of friends. But the zone is also "wild" in the sense that anyone who has the good fortune to share his or her space with another species may come to understand that a dog or a cat or a horse, for example, could easily become wild again and that these animals blur the line between wild and domestic, allowing one to feel and experience a wilderness that still beckons. I imagine this reconfigured *domus* as a sort of negotiation with borders, wild and domestic, perhaps even a border crossing into a frontier space that continuously recalls the wild as we simultaneously remain sheltered from abandonment and suffering.

Exploitation, cruelty, or neglect can and sadly all too frequently do happen in any cohabitated space. The stories examined in this book, however, offer positive explorations of nonconventional forms of intimacy between different creatures and between different kinds of creatures.

What remains of this "afterword" points to a "foreword" to another work: the sense that trauma is what underlies the creation of such alternative lifestyles. Although trauma has not been the focus here, all the authors in this study suffer (and suffered) from a deeply felt sense of loss that is overdetermined and that points to the trauma of sexuality (Freud and de Lauretis), the trauma of major world and life catastrophes such as war and holocausts, and the trauma of experiencing ourselves as beings distinct from nature—all of which these authors have shown and remarked upon. Nothing more poignantly brings to mind the drastic consequences of humans' alienation from the rest of nature than repeated ecological disasters such as the BP oil spill in the Gulf of Mexico, where human and nonhuman lives are destroyed and entire ecosystems imperiled. Perhaps a polymorphous domesticity is one way to bridge the chasm that continues to prevail in our culture, as shown by the practices of its dominant entities, such as corporations, whose primary concern is profit and not the "small" people (of "small" businesses) or the animals it has killed. My four writers, in their own ways, confronted trauma and found creative ways of expressing a desired polymorphous world, one among many possibilities, and with it a future that would respect life and the earth.

Notes

INTRODUCTION

The chapter epigraph is from Gertrude Stein, *Paris, France* (New York: Charles Scribner's Sons, 1940), 94–95.

1. Juliana Schiesari, *Beasts and Beauties: Animals, Gender and Domestication in the Italian Renaissance* (Toronto: University of Toronto Press, 2010).

2. Francesco Barbaro, "On Wifely Duties," trans. Benjamin G. Kohl, in *The Earthly Republic: Italian Humanism on Government and Society,* ed. Benjamin Kohl and Ronald G. Witt (Philadelphia: University of Pennsylvania Press, 1978), 189–288; Leon-Battista Alberti, *I libri di famiglia,* trans. Renee Neu Watkins (Columbia South Carolina: University of South Carolina Press, 1969).

3. Stein, *Paris, France,* 94–95.

4. For an excellent source on witchcraft in Europe, see Alan C. Kors and Edward Peters, eds., *Witchcraft in Europe: A Documentary History, 1100–1700* (Philadelphia: University of Pennsylvania Press, 1972).

5. Carla Freccero, "Figural Historiography: Dogs, Humans, and Cynathropic Becomings," in *Comparatively Queer: Interrogating Identities across Time and Cultures,* ed. Jarrod Hayes, Margaret R. Higonnet, and William J. Spurlin (New York: Palgrave Macmillan, 2010), 45–67.

6. See ibid.

7. See Juliana Schiesari, "Bitches and Queens: Pets and Perversion at the Court of France's Henri III," in *Renaissance Beasts: Of Animals and Other Wonderful Creatures,* ed. Erica Fudge (Urbana: University of Illinois Press, 2004), 38–58. There I argue that the beastliness of desire has been a staple in literary texts since at least Plato. Further, it retains its fascination across a number of literary texts throughout Western literature, even going back as far as the ancient poems and epigrams in Maximus Planudes's *Greek Anthology*

(first published in Florence in 1994). Indeed, one can argue that "Beauty and Beast" is one of the countless narratives, reconfigured here in the authors I study, who phrase both the fear and attraction of desire as a confrontation with the nonhuman and rephrase that desire as a "polymorphous community" that represents and eschews the eroticism of the encounter and thus dispels any terror while underscoring pleasure.

Another example of the "perverse" power of alternative lifestyles to create paradigmatic shifts in thinking is the poignant moment in J.M. Coetzee's novel *Disgrace* when his lesbian daughter, who lives in rural South Africa and looks after unwanted dogs, says to her father (a disgraced professor), "You think I ought to be doing something better with my life.... You think I ought to be painting still lifes or teaching myself Russian. You do not approve of friends like Bev and Bill Shaw because they are not going to lead me to a higher life." He responds, "That is not true, Lucy." And she replies, "But it is true. They are not going to lead me to a higher life, and the reason is, there is no higher life. This is the only life there is. Which we share with animals.... To share some of our human privilege with the beasts. I do not want to come back in another existence as a dog or a pig and have to live as dogs or pigs live under us." J.M. Coetzee, *Disgrace* (New York: Penguin Books, 2000), 74.

Lucy's remark and Coetzee's novel help us reflect on the meaning of what it means to be a human being in a world where dominance of one group, one race, or one species over another is mindlessly reproduced even at the academic level of notions of a "higher" and "lower" forms of being. The "colonized" body haunts this text not only in terms of its relation to postapartheid South Africa but also in terms of gender and species.

8. For the "classic" definition of *polymorphism*, see Sigmund Freud, "Infantile Sexuality," in *The Standard Edition of the Complete Psychological Works of Sigmund Freud*, ed. James Strachey, vol. 7 (London: Hogarth Press, 1953), 191–93. For Freud, children "under the influence of seduction can become polymorphously perverse, and can be led into all kinds of sexual irregularities. This shows that an aptitude for this is innately present in their disposition." My use of polymorphism is akin to its Freudian revision by Deleuze and Guattari in *Anti-Oedipus* (New York: Viking, 1977), and by Judith Butler, particularly in her *Gender Trouble: Feminism and the Subversion of Identity* (New York: Routledge, 2006). These theorists revise Freud's concept of polymorphism as an aberrant infantile behavior and see it rather as a creative challenge and resistance to Freud's Oedipal concept.

9. Gilles Deleuze and Felix Guattari, *A Thousand Plateaus: Capitalism and Schizophrenia II*, trans. Brian Massumi (Minneapolis: University of Minnesota Press, 1987), 237. For an excellent discussion of "*devenir-animal*" as undoing the identity subject of humanism and radically suggesting that the call comes from the animal itself, see Steve Baker, *The Postmodern Animal* (London: Reaktion Books, 2000), 102–13.

10. For the postmodern philosophical discussion on the nonhuman, see Baker, *Postmodern Animal;* Jacques Derrida, *L'animal autobiographique: Autour de Jacques Derrida*, ed. Marie-Louise Mallet (Paris: Galilée, 1999) and *L'animal que donc je suis* (Paris: Galilée, 2006); Gilles Deleuze and Félix

Guattari, *A Thousand Plateaus: Capitalism and Schizophrenia*, trans. Brian Massumi (London: Athlone Press, 1988); Jean-François Lyotard, *The Inhuman*, trans. Geoff Bennington and Rachel Bowlby (Stanford: Stanford University Press, 1991); Giorgio Agamben, *The Open: Man and Animal*, trans. Kevin Attell (Stanford: Stanford University Press, 2004); Leonard Lawler, *This Is Not Sufficient: An Essay on Animality and Human Nature in Derrida* (New York: Columbia University Press, 2007).

11. Among the many key players here we must of course count Peter Singer (*Animal Liberation* [New York: HarperCollins, 1975] and his edited volume *In Defense of Animals: The Second Wave* [Oxford: Basil Blackwell, 2006]) and Tom Regan ("The Case for Animal Rights," in *In Defense of Animals*, ed. Peter Singer [New York: Harper and Row, 1985], 13–27), as well as Paola Cavalieri (*The Animal Question: Why Nonhuman Animals Deserve Human Rights* [New York: Oxford University Press, 2001]) and Martha Nussbaum and Cass Sunstein (coeditors of *Animal Rights: Current Debates and New Directions* [Oxford: Oxford University Press, 2004]).

12. Vicki Hearne, *Adam's Task: Calling Animals by Name* (New York: Knopf, 1986) and *Bandit: Dossier of a Dangerous Dog* (New York: HarperCollins, 1991); Jeffrey Masson, *When Elephants Weep: The Emotional Lives of Animals* (New York: Delacorte Press, 1995); Marc Bekoff, *The Emotional Lives of Animals* (Novato, CA: New World Library, 2007); Marian Stamp Dawkins, *Through Our Eyes Only: The Search for Animal Consciousness* (Oxford: Oxford University Press, 1998).

13. See especially Harriet Ritvo, *The Animal Estate: The English and Other Creatures in the Victorian Age* (Cambridge, MA: Harvard University Press, 1987); James Serpell, *In the Company of Animals: A Study of Human-Animal Relationships* (Cambridge: Cambridge University Press, 1996); Midas Dekkers, *Dearest Pet: On Bestiality*, trans. Paul Vincent (London: Verso, 1994); John Simons, *Animal Rights and the Politics of Literary Representation* (Houndmills: Palgrave, 2002); and Baker, *Postmodern Animal*.

14. Carol J. Adams, *The Sexual Politics of Meat: A Feminist-Vegetarian Critical Theory* (New York: Continuum, 1990), and Carol J. Adams and Josephine Donovan, eds., *Animals and Women: Feminist Theoretical Explorations* (Durham: Duke University Press, 1995); Mary Midgley, *Animals and Why They Matter* (Harmondsworth: Penguin Books, 1983).

15. Donna Haraway, *Primate Visions: Gender, Race, and Nature in the World of Modern Science* (New York: Routledge, 1989), *The Companion Species Manifesto: Dogs, People, and Significant Otherness* (Chicago: Prickly Paradigm Press, 2003), and *When Species Meet* (Minneapolis: University of Minnesota Press, 2008); Carey Wolfe, *Animal Rites: American Culture, the Discourse of Species, and Posthumanist Theory* (Chicago: University of Chicago Press, 2003), and his edited volume *Zoontologies: The Question of the Animal* (Minneapolis: University of Minnesota Press, 2003).

16. See Brian Cummings, "Animal Passions and Human Sciences," in *At the Borders of the Human: Beasts, Bodies and Natural Philosophy in the Early Modern Period*, ed. Erica Fudge, Susan Wiseman, and Ruth Gilbert (New York: Palgrave Macmillan, 2002), 26–50.

17. Michel de Montaigne, *The Complete Essays,* trans. Donald M. Frame (Stanford: Stanford University Press, 1958), 331; cf. George Boas, *The Happy Beast in French Thought of the Seventeenth Century* (New York: Octagon Books, 1966) for more such examples.

18. Simons, *Animal Rights,* 116–21. I agree with much of his argument. The major flaw, however, in his work is his peculiar Anglocentric bias. Despite his contention, continental Europe has also had a long and vital tradition of lobbying for animals. In Italy, for example, one must account for the strong philosophical and spiritual legacy of St. Francis of Assisi as patron of animals. Simons's assumption of a Protestant/Catholic difference in attitudes toward animals seems equally unjustified. I dare say that as many Protestants as Catholics feel justified in pursuing a scientific imperative to pitilessly dissect and experiment on animals. It seems that it is Christianity that is bad for animals, whether it is Catholic or Protestant!

19. Robert W. Mitchell, Nicholas S. Thompson, and H. Lyn Miles, eds., *Anthropomorphism, Anecdotes, and Animals* (Albany: State University of New York Press), esp. 3–11.

20. Friedrich Nietzsche, "On Truth and Falsity in an Extra-Moral Sense," in *The Portable Nietzsche,* ed. and trans. Walter Kaufman (New York: Norton, 1965).

21. See Sigmund Freud's enduring work on projection and introjection.

22. See James A. Serpell's provocative article "Anthropomorphism and Anthropomorphic Selection—Beyond the "Cute Response,'" *Society and Animals* 10, no. 4 (2002): 437–54. The horse-training methods and insights of Monty Roberts offer another practical case in point of such "eccentric" anthropomorphism.

23. J.R. Ackerley, "I Am a Beast," *Orient West* 9, no. 2 (1964): 67–72. Also see Juliana Schiesari, "J.R. Ackerley e le bestie della Malinconia," in *Arcipelago malinconia,* ed. Biancamaria Frabotta (Rome: Donizelli, 2001), 51–60. A most enticing "anthropomorphic" moment is recounted by Ackerley, in his semiautobiographical book *My Dog Tulip (*New York: New York Review of Books, 1965), 61:

> There came a day, however, when we were walking in Wimbledon woods and she suddenly added my urine, which I had been obliged to void, to the other privileged objects of her social attention. How touched I was! How honored I felt! "Oh, Tulip! Thank you," I said.
>
> And now she always does it. No matter how preoccupied her mind may be with other things, such as rabbiting, she will always turn back, before following me, to the place where she saw me relieve myself—for nothing that I do escapes her—to sprinkle her own drops upon mine. So I feel that if ever there were differences between us they are washed out now. *I feel a proper dog.* (emphasis mine)

24. Carole Law Trachy, *The Mythology of Artemis and Her Role in Greek Popular Religion* (Ann Arbor: UMI, 1977), 3; Schiesari, *Beasts and Beauties,* ch. 6. Also see Matt Cartmill's *A View to a Death in the Morning: Hunting and Nature throughout History* (Cambridge, MA: Harvard University Press, 1993), 28–51, for a discussion of the mythical Artemis/Diana as an empowering figure for women and its revisionist history during the Middle Ages and Renaissance.

25. See Freccero, "Figural Historiography."

26. See Trachy, *Mythology of Artemis,* 31. As early as the tenth-century *Canon Episcopi,* warnings are uttered about "some wicked women, perverted by the Devil, seduced by illusions and phantasms of demons, [who] believe and profess themselves, in the hours of the night, to ride upon certain beasts with Diana, the goddess of pagans, and an innumerable multitude of women, and in the silence of the dead of the night to traverse great spaces of earth, and to obey her commands as of their mistress, and to be summoned to her service on certain nights" (quoted on 127). That text further warns that such "false opinions" are believed by "an innumerable multitude" who are thus at risk of leaving the faith and embracing the ways of the pagans. The matter was serious enough that this passage was incorporated by Gratian into the text of canon law and later reappeared verbatim in Heinrich Kramer and James Sprenger's infamous *Malleus Maleficarum* of 1484, which was used as an aid to inquisitors conducting the witch trials of the early modern era. Clearly, the threat of multitudes of women and animals congregating at night to honor Diana, goddess of the moon, posed a direct challenge to Catholic authority, as it testified to the persistence of a popular pagan cult—and a feminocentric one at that!—from antiquity well into modern times.

27. See Trachy, *Mythology of Artemis,* 31.

28. Ibid., 33.

1. RE-VISIONS OF DIANA IN EDITH WHARTON

1. The term *lurking feminism* was first applied to Wharton's work by Blake Nevius in his classic *Edith Wharton: A Study of Her Fiction* (Berkeley: University of California Press, 1953), 185, and has been reenergized by Jenni Dyman in her *Lurking Feminism: The Ghost Stories of Edith Wharton* (New York: Peter Lang, 1996).

2. See ch. 1 of Schiesari, *Beasts and Beauties,* titled "Jewels of Women."

3. Quoted in Dyman, *Lurking Feminism,* 78.

4. Quoted in ibid. In *Edith Wharton's Prisoners of Shame* (London: Palgrave, 1991), Lev Raphael comments on Wharton's "deep and lifelong identification with small animals, particularly dogs," as being especially revealing since, as Darwin first noted, "the dog is the most sociophilic of animals, and characteristically the most readily observed to display the head and eyes lowered in shame. Wharton describes herself as feeling in touch with the unexpressed feelings of small animals, and 'possessed by a haunting consciousness of [their] sufferings longing to protect them against cruelty and pain.' How 'safe and sheltered,' then, was her childhood really, if she was drawn towards the helpless and felt so herself?" (quoted in Dyman, *Lurking Feminism,* 90).

5. Sandra M. Gilbert and Susan Gubar, "Angel of Devastation: Edith Wharton on the Arts of the Enslaved," in *Sex Changes,* vol. 2 of *No Man's Land: The Place of the Woman Writer in the Twentieth Century* (New Haven: Yale University Press, 1989), 159–64.

6. The poem "Artemis and Actaeon" appears as the lead lyric in Edith Wharton, *Artemis to Actaeon and Other Verse* (New York: Charles Scribner's Sons, 1909), 3–6.

7. "Kerfol," in *The Selected Stories of Edith Wharton,* ed. R.W.B. Lewis (New York: Charles Scribner's Sons, 1991), 210. All subsequent page citations to this work are to this edition and are given parenthetically in the text.

8. See Teresa de Lauretis's brilliant analysis of Barnes in her *Freud's Drive: Psychoanalysis, Literature and Film* (New York: Palgrave Macmillan, 2008), 133.

9. Ibid., 118.

10. Ibid., 119.

11. Ibid., 137.

12. Djuna Barnes, *Nightwood* (New York: Harcourt, Brace, 1937), 70. All further page citations to this work are to this edition and are given parenthetically in the text.

13. Although most of Georges Bataille's works were not published in book form till much later, including *L'erotisme* (Paris: Minuit, 1957), translated by Mary Dallwood as *Death and Sensuality: A Study of Eroticism and the Taboo* (New York: Waller, 1962), many of his controversial ideas were already circulating in articles. For a representative selection, see *Visions of Excess: Selected Writings, 1927–1939,* ed. and trans. Allan Stoekl (Minneapolis: University of Minnesota Press, 1985).

14. Jane Marcus, "Laughing at Leviticus: *Nightwood* as a Woman's Circus Epic," in *Silence and Power: A Reevaluation of Djuna Barnes,* ed. Mary Lynn Broe (Carbondale: Southern Illinois University Press, 1991), 249. Marcus astutely observes also that "one of *Nightwood's* most fascinating aspects is that it has more animal characters than people" (248).

15. See Max Horhheimer and Theodor Adorno's suggestive discussion in this regard, "Man and Animal," in *Dialectic of Enlightenment,* trans. John Cumming (New York: Seabury Press, 1972), 245–55: "The idea of man in European history is expressed in the way in which he is distinguished from the animal."

16. I recall here Vicki Hearne's powerful critique of anthropocentrism and anthropomorphism in *Adam's Task.* Kenneth Burke's classic reading of *Nightwood,* "Version, Con-, Per-, and In-: Thoughts on Djuna Barnes's Novel *Nightwood,*" in *Language as Symbolic Action* (Berkeley: University of California Press, 1968), 240–53, as motivated by a rhetoric of "tragic dignification" and "transcendence downward," remains resolutely anthropocentric in this sense. For if Robin's "enigmatic communion with a dog" is really but an inverted or perverted way of approaching God, then "dog" and "God" are but signs of each other (as the two words are themselves mirror images of each other: d-o-g = g-o-d). Whatever "dog" might mean in the here and now is then quickly transcoded to the transcendental register of the divine.

17. Marcus likewise notes the resonances of the Diana myth in *Nightwood* but assimilates the goddess to the character of Robin, whom she describes as "the androgynous ideal, the archetype of the sacred virgin Diana, a feminist version of the Noble Savage; *Nightwood* is her 'sacred grove'" ("Laughing at Leviticus," 248). At other places in her otherwise magnificent analysis, however, she refrains from directly identifying Robin with Diana, speaking rather of an "association with the virgin Diana of Ephesus" (241), or even edging closer to

my own reading of the last scene as Robin's coming home to the composite Diana/Madonna figure that is Nora: "Robin Vote [says] 'no' to marriage, 'no' to motherhood, 'no' to monogamous lesbianism. Robin's 'no' is a preverbal, prepatriarchal, primitive bark—as the novel ends in America and she ritually acts the bear before her Madonna-Artemis, goddess of autonomous sexuality, owner of her body and her self" (230). What might appear at first to be a confusion of symbols on the part of a critic so rigorously attentive to detail can be resolved if we recall my discussion, in *Beasts and Beauties,* of the double lineage and double iconography of Diana, split between patriarchally legitimate and illegitimate views of the deity's survival in Western culture after the end of antiquity.

2. COLETTE AT HOME

1. Colette, *Oeuvres,* ed. Claude Pichois et al. (Paris: Gallimard, 1984–91), 3:1041. All subsequent citations to this work, hereafter abbreviated as O, will be given parenthetically in the text by volume and page number. So far, only three volumes of this Pléiade critical edition have been published. All references to works of Colette *not* included in the Pléiade edition will be to the *Oeuvres complètes de Colette* (Paris: Le Fleuron, 1949–50) and will be indicated by the initials *OC* plus the relevant volume and page numbers. Since there is no equivalent critical edition in English, translated texts will be cited individually in the notes on first mention, then indicated parenthetically in the text by page number alone after the French reference followed by a slash. All uncredited translations are my own.

2. *My Apprenticeships,* trans. Helen Beauclerk (New York: Farrar, Straus and Giroux, 1978), 84–85; translation modified.

3. Colette, interview by Jean de La Hire, in his *Ménages d'artiste: Willy et Colette* (Paris: Bibliothèque indépendante d'édition, 1903), 269, quoted in O, 1:1287.

4. Colette and Jammes knew each other only by their exchange of letters, which have been edited by Robert Mallet under the title *Une amitié inattendue: Correspondance de Colette et de Francis Jammes* (Paris: Editions Emile-Paul Frères, 1945).

5. The original of this painting hangs in the Barcelona Museum of Modern Art.

6. Such enthusiastic proclamations as those of Jean de la Hire, who attributed to Colette "la gloire redoubtable et rare de créer un genre" (*Ménages d'artiste,* 126), and Rachilde, in her April 1904 review for the *Mercure de France,* recall Catulle Mendès's famous remarks, reproduced in *My Apprenticeships,* about Colette having invented a new literary "type" in the character of Claudine (O, 3:1013/46). Despite the novelty of her animal dialogues at the time they appeared in print, Colette draws on a long tradition of talking pets in literature, described, for example, by Theodore Ziolkowski's "Talking Dogs: The Caninization of Literature," in *Varieties of Literary Thematics* (Princeton: Princeton University Press, 1983), 86–122.

7. *O*, 1:960; "A Fable: The Tendrils of the Vine," trans. Herma Briffault, in *The Collected Stories of Colette*, ed. Robert Phelps (New York: Farrar, Straus, Giroux, 1983), 101; trans. modified.

8. A thorough manuscript and publishing history as well as the complete set of variants can be consulted in *O*, 1:1530–55.

9. *O*, 1:997; "Toby-Dog Speaks," from *Creature Conversations*, in *Creatures Great and Small*, trans. Enid McLeod (London: Martin Secker and Warburg, 1951), 129, trans. modified.

10. *O*, 1:989. Interestingly, and despite what I believe to be the crucial import of this story to Colette's work as a whole, it appears to have remained untranslated and is curiously absent from McLeod's *Creatures Great and Small*.

11. Colette's deepening sense of loss can be charted by the sale of the family home in Saint-Sauveur after her father's bankruptcy in 1890, the death of her mother in 1912, and the loss even of that marvelously substitutive Monts-Baucons in 1908, when a vindictive Willy repossessed it to pay off his massive debts and perhaps symbolically to punish Colette's rediscovery of herself in a location that would lead her back to the meaning of her maternal home—and would enable her to write about it with the confidence finally to drop "Willy" from her pen name!

12. The manuscript evidence suggests that Colette began writing what would become *My Mother's House* with the intention of describing the land of her childhood and that only through the writing process did she come to realize the central importance of "the personage who, little by little, has dominated [her] work: the personage of [her] mother." Preface to *My Mother's House*, trans. Una Vicenzo Troubridge and Enid McLeod, new rev. ed. (London: Secker and Warburg, 1969), xix. (This edition is used for the translations from *My Mother's House* that follow.)

13. "Mothers and Children," trans. Herma Briffault, in *The Earthly Paradise: An Autobiography Drawn from Her Lifetime Writings*, ed. Robert Phelps (New York: Farrar, Straus and Giroux, 1966), 31.

14. Interestingly enough, "Bâ-Tou" and four other "animal stories" are inexplicably absent from the English translation of *My Mother's House*. Nor, as far as I can tell, have they been translated elsewhere, as eloquent a testimony as any to the critical marginalization of this entire strand of Colette's writing (see note 17 below).

15. The animal stories from *Prisons et paradis* have also apparently never been translated, though other texts from that collection have appeared in various anthologies of Colette stories.

16. *Break of Day*, trans. Enid McLeod (repr., New York: Farrar, Strauss and Giroux, 1966), 44.

17. While countless critics mention Colette's well-known love for animals, only two have dealt with this clearly central aspect of Colette's work in any systematic fashion: Régine Detambel's *Colette: Comme une flore, comme un zoo* (Paris: Stock, 1997) is helpful mainly as a critical compilation of animal (and floral) imagery in Colette's fiction; Mihailo B. Pavlovic's *Sidonie-Gabrielle Colette: Le monde animal dans sa vie et dans sa création littéraire* (Belgrade: Filoloski Fakultet Beogradskrog Univerziteta, 1970) is a published dissertation,

very thorough but limiting itself to an essentially thematic approach. The best short treatment of the theme is to be found in Elaine Marks, *Colette* (New Brunswick: Rutgers University Press, 1960), 186–95.

18. *Times Literary Supplement,* August 10, 1933
19. *Times Literary Supplement,* October 16, 1953.
20. Pierre Bost, "La chatte," *L'Europe nouvelle,* July 8, 1933.
21. Germaine Beaumont, introduction to *Colette par elle-même,* by Germaine Beaumont and André Parinaud (Paris: Seuil, n.d.), 30.
22. Joan Hinde Stewart, *Colette,* updated ed. (New York: Twayne, 1996), 63–65.
23. Marks, *Colette,* 190–92.
24. Gonzague Truc, *Madame Colette* (Paris: Corrêa, 1941), 145.
25. Margaret M. Callander, *Colette: Le blé en herbe and La chatte,* Critical Guides to French Texts 91 (London: Grants and Cutler, 1992), 53.
26. Maurice Goudeket, *Près de Colette* (Paris: Flammarion, 1956), 39; *Close to Colette: An Intimate Portrait of a Woman of Genius,* introd. and trans. Harold Nicolson (New York: Farrar, Straus and Cudahy, 1957), 34.
27. Colette, *La fanal bleu, OC,* 14:119; *The Blue Lantern,* trans. Roger Senhouse (New York: Farrar, Straus and Giroux), 136.
28. Colette, *L'étoile vesper, OC,* 13:268; *The Evening Star: Recollections,* trans. David Le Vay (London: Peter Owen, 1973), 89.

3. ROMANCING THE BEAST

1. E.M. Forster, *Selected Letters,* quoted in Peter Parker, *Ackerley: A Life of J.R. Ackerley* (London: Constable, 1989), 263.
2. See Walter Kendrick, "Heavy Petting: J.R. Ackerley Goes to the Dogs," *Village Voice Literary Supplement,* October 1990, 14–15.
3. J.R. Ackerley, *We Think the World of You* (New York: NYRB Classics, 2000), 28. All subsequent citations are to this edition and are given parenthetically in the text.
4. Parker, *Ackerley,* 323.
5. Jean-François Lyotard, *The Differend: Phrases in Dispute* (Minneapolis: University of Minnesota Press, 1988), 28.
6. J.R. Ackerley, *My Sister and Myself: The Diaries of J.R. Ackerley,* ed. Francis King (London: Hutchinson, 1982).
7. J.R. Ackerley, *My Dog Tulip* (New York: New York Review of Books, 1965), 59. All subsequent citations to this work are to this edition and are given parenthetically in the text.
8. Parker, *Ackerley,* 322–23.
9. Ibid.
10. J.R. Ackerley to Geoffrey Gorer, in ibid., 118–19.
11. J.R. Ackerley, *My Father and Myself* (New York: New York Review of Books, 1968), 129–30. All subsequent citations to this work are given parenthetically in the text.
12. Quoted in Parker, *Ackerley,* 119, emphasis in text.

13. See "Note to Freud," *Three Essays,* Laplanche; de Lauretis, *Freud's Drive,* etc.

14. See Della Porta,

15. Ackerley, "I Am a Beast," 67. All subsequent citations to this work are given parenthetically in the text.

16. On Renaissance theriophily, the best reference remains George Boas's classic, *The Happy Beast.*

Bibliography

Ackerley, J.R. "I Am a Beast." *Orient West* 9, no. 2 (1964): 67–72.
———. *My Dog Tulip*. New York: New York Review of Books, 1965.
———. *My Father and Myself*. New York: New York Review of Books, 1968.
———. *My Sister and Myself: The Diaries of J.R. Ackerley*. Ed. Francis King. London: Hutchinson, 1982.
———. *We Think the World of You*. New York: NYRB Classics, 2000.
Adams, Carol J. *The Sexual Politics of Meat: A Feminist-Vegetarian Critical Theory*. New York: Continuum, 1990.
Adams, Carol J., and Josephine Donovan, eds. *Animals and Women: Feminist Theoretical Explorations*. Durham: Duke University Press, 1995.
Agamben, Giorgio. *The Open: Man and Animal*. Trans. Kevin Attell. Stanford: Stanford University Press, 2004.
Alberti, Leon-Battista. *I libri di famiglia*. Trans. Renee Neu Watkins. Columbia: University of South Carolina Press, 1969.
Baker, Steve. *The Postmodern Animal*. London: Reaktion Books, 2000.
Barbaro, Francesco. "On Wifely Duties." Trans. Benjamin G. Kohl. In *The Earthly Republic: Italian Humanism on Government and Society*, ed. Benjamin Kohl and Ronald G. Witt, 189–288. Philadelphia: University of Pennsylvania Press, 1978.
Barnes, Djuna. *Nightwood*. New York: Harcourt, Brace, 1937.
Bataille, Georges. *L'erotisme*. Paris: Minuit, 1957. Translated by Mary Dallwood as *Death and Sensuality: A Study of Eroticism and the Taboo* (New York: Waller, 1962).
———. *Visions of Excess: Selected Writings, 1927–1939*. Ed. and trans. Allan Stoekl. Minneapolis: University of Minnesota Press, 1985.
Beaumont, Germaine, and André Parinaud, eds. *Colette par elle-même*. Paris: Seuil.

Bekoff, Marc. *The Emotional Lives of Animals*. Novato, CA: New World Library, 2007.
Boas, George. *The Happy Beast in French Thought of the Seventeenth Century*. New York: Octagon Books, 1966.
Burke, Kenneth. "Version, Con-, Per-, and In-: Thoughts on Djuna Barnes's Novel *Nightwood*." In *Language as Symbolic Action*, 240–53. Berkeley: University of California Press, 1968.
Butler, Judith. *Gender Trouble: Feminism and the Subversion of Identity*. New York: Routledge, 2006.
Callander, Margaret M. *Colette: Le blé en herbe and La chatte*. Critical Guides to French Texts 91. London: Grants and Cutler, 1992.
Cartmill, Matt. *A View to a Death in the Morning: Hunting and Nature throughout History*. Cambridge, MA: Harvard University Press, 1993.
Cavalieri, Paola. *The Animal Question: Why Nonhuman Animals Deserve Human Rights*. New York: Oxford University Press, 2001.
Coetzee, J.M. *Disgrace*. New York: Penguin Books, 2000.
Colette. *Une amitié inattendue: Correspondance de Colette et de Francis Jammes*. Ed. Robert Mallet. Paris: Editions Emile-Paul Frères, 1945.
———. *The Blue Lantern*. Trans. Roger Senhouse. New York: Farrar, Straus and Giroux.
———. *Break of Day*. Trans. Enid McLeod. New York: Farrar, Straus and Giroux, 1966.
———. *Creature Conversations*. In *Creatures Great and Small*, trans. Enid McLeod. London: Martin Secker and Warburg, 1951.
———. *The Evening Star: Recollections*. Trans. David Le Vay. London: Peter Owen, 1973.
———. "A Fable: The Tendrils of the Vine." Trans. Herma Briffault. In *The Collected Stories of Colette*, ed. Robert Phelps, trans. Matthew Ward et al. New York: Farrar, Straus, Giroux, 1983.
———. Interview by Jean de La Hire. In *Ménages d'artiste: Willy et Colette*. Paris: Bibliothèque indépendante d'édition, 1903.
———. "Mothers and Children." Trans. Herma Briffault. In *The Earthly Paradise: An Autobiography Drawn from Her Lifetime Writings*, ed. Robert Phelps. New York: Farrar, Strauss and Giroux, 1966.
———. *My Apprenticeships*. Trans. Helen Beauclerk. New York: Farrar, Straus and Giroux, 1978.
———. *My Mother's House*. Trans. Una Vicenzo Troubridge and Enid McLeod. New rev. ed. London: Secker and Warburg, 1969.
———. *Oeuvres*. Ed. Claude Pichois et al. Paris: Gallimard, 1984–91.
———. *Oeuvres complètes de Colette*. Ed. Maurice Goudeket. Paris: Le Fleuron, 1949–50.
Cummings, Brian. "Animal Passions and Human Sciences." In *At the Borders of the Human: Beasts, Bodies and Natural Philosophy in the Early Modern Period*, ed. Erica Fudge, Susan Wiseman, and Ruth Gilbert, 26–50. New York: Palgrave Macmillan, 2002.
Dekkers, Midas. *Dearest Pet: On Bestiality*. Trans. Paul Vincent. London: Verso, 1994.

de Lauretis, Teresa. *Freud's Drive: Psychoanalysis, Literature and Film*. New York: Palgrave Macmillan, 2008.
Deleuze, Gilles, and Félix Guattari. *Anti-Oedipus*. New York: Viking, 1977.
———. *A Thousand Plateaus: Capitalism and Schizophrenia*. Trans. Brian Massumi. London: Athlone Press, 1988.
———. *A Thousand Plateaus: Capitalism and Schizophrenia II*. Trans. Brian Massumi. Minneapolis: University of Minnesota Press, 1987.
Derrida, Jacques. *L'animal autobiographique: Autour de Jacques Derrida*. Ed. Marie-Louise Mallet. Paris: Galilée, 1999.
———. *L'animal que donc je suis*. Paris: Galilée, 2006.
Detambel, Régine. *Colette: Comme une flore, comme un zoo*. Paris: Stock, 1997.
Dyman, Jenni. *Lurking Feminism: The Ghost Stories of Edith Wharton*. New York: Peter Lang, 1996.
Freccero, Carla. "Figural Historiography: Dogs, Humans, and Cyanthropic Becomings." In *Comparatively Queer*, ed. Jarrod Hayes, Margaret Higonne, and William J. Spurlin, 45–67. New York: Palgrave Macmillan, 2010.
Freud, Sigmund. "Infantile Sexuality." In *The Standard Edition of the Complete Psychological Works of Sigmund Freud*, ed. James Strachey, vol. 7. London: Hogarth Press, 1953.
———. *Three Essays on Sexuality*. In *The Standard Edition of the Complete Psychological Works of Sigmund Freud*, ed. James Strachey, vol. 7. London: Hogarth Press, 1953.
Gilbert, Sandra M., and Susan Gubar. "Angel of Devastation: Edith Wharton on the Arts of the Enslaved." In *Sex Changes*, vol. 2 of *No Man's Land: The Place of the Woman Writer in the Twentieth Century*, 159–64. New Haven: Yale University Press, 1989.
Goudeket, Maurice. *Close to Colette: An Intimate Portrait of a Woman of Genius*. Introd. and trans. Harold Nicolson. New York: Farrar, Straus, and Cudahy, 1957.
———. *Près de Colette*. Paris: Flammarion, 1956.
Haraway, Donna. *The Companion Species Manifesto: Dogs, People, and Significant Otherness*. Chicago: Prickly Paradigm Press, 2003.
———. *Primate Visions: Gender, Race, and Nature in the World of Modern Science*. New York: Routledge, 1989.
———. *When Species Meet*. Minneapolis: University of Minnesota Press, 2008.
Hearne, Vicki. *Adam's Task: Calling Animals by Name*. New York: Knopf, 1986.
———. *Bandit: Dossier of a Dangerous Dog*. New York: HarperCollins, 1991.
Horkheimer, Max, and Theodor Adorno. "Man and Animal." In *Dialectic of Enlightenment*, trans. John Cumming, 245–55. New York: Seabury Press, 1972.
Kendrick, Walter. "Heavy Petting: J.R. Ackerley Goes to the Dogs." *Village Voice Literary Supplement*, October 1990, 14–15.
Kors, Alan C., and Edward Peters, eds. *Witchcraft in Europe: A Documentary History, 1100–1700*. Philadelphia: University of Pennsylvania Press, 1972.

Lawler, Leonard. *This Is Not Sufficient: An Essay on Animality and Human Nature in Derrida.* New York: Columbia University Press, 2007.
Lyotard, Jean-François. *The Differend: Phrases in Dispute.* Minneapolis: University of Minnesota Press, 1988.
———. *The Inhuman.* Trans. Geoff Bennington and Rachel Bowlby. Stanford: Stanford University Press, 1991.
Marcus, Jane. "Laughing at Leviticus: *Nightwood* as a Woman's Circus Epic." In *Silence and Power: A Reevaluation of Djuna Barnes,* ed. Mary Lynn Broe, 221–51. Carbondale: Southern Illinois University Press, 1991.
Marks, Elaine. *Colette.* New Brunswick: Rutgers University Press, 1960.
Masson, Jeffrey. *When Elephants Weep: The Emotional Lives of Animals.* New York: Delacorte Press, 1995.
Midgley, Mary. *Animals and Why They Matter.* Harmondsworth: Penguin Books, 1983.
Mitchell, Robert W., Nicholas S. Thompson, and H. Lyn Miles, eds. *Anthropomorphism, Anecdotes, and Animals.* Albany: State University of New York Press.
Montaigne, Michel de. *The Complete Essays.* Trans. Donald M. Frame. Stanford: Stanford University Press, 1958.
Nevius, Blake. *Edith Wharton: A Study of Her Fiction.* Berkeley: University of California Press, 1953.
Nietzsche, Friedrich. "On Truth and Falsity in an Extra-Moral Sense." In *The Portable Nietzsche,* ed. and trans. Walter Kaufman, 42–47. New York: Norton, 1965.
Nussbaum, Martha, and Cass Sunstein, eds. *Animal Rights: Current Debates and New Directions.* Oxford: Oxford University Press, 2004.
Parker, Peter. *Ackerley: A Life of J R. Ackerley.* London: Constable, 1989.
Pavlovic, Mihailo B. *Sidonie-Gabrielle Colette: Le monde animal dans sa vie et dans sa création littéraire.* Belgrade: Filoloski Fakultet Beogradskrog Univerziteta, 1970.
Raphael, Lev. *Edith Wharton's Prisoners of Shame.* London: Palgrave, 1991.
Regan, Tom. "The Case for Animal Rights." In *In Defense of Animals,* ed. Peter Singer, 13–27. New York: Harper and Row, 1985.
Ritvo, Harriet. *The Animal Estate: The English and Other Creatures in the Victorian Age.* Cambridge, MA: Harvard University Press, 1987.
Schiesari, Juliana. *Beasts and Beauties: Animals, Gender and Domestication in the Italian Renaissance.* Toronto: University of Toronto Press, 2010.
———. "Bitches and Queens: Pets and Perversion at the Court of France's Henri III." In *Renaissance Beasts: Of Animals and Other Wonderful Creatures,* ed. Erica Fudge, 38–58. Urbana: University of Illinois Press, 2004.
———. "J.R. Ackerley e le bestie della Malinconia." In *Arcipelago malinconia,* ed. Biancamaria Frabotta, 51–60. Rome: Donizelli, 2001.
Serpell, James. "Anthropomorphism and Anthropomorphic Selection: Beyond the 'Cute Response.'{hrs}" *Society and Animals* 10, no. 4 (2002): 437–54.
———. *In the Company of Animals: A Study of Human-Animal Relationships.* Cambridge: Cambridge University Press, 1996.

Simons, John. *Animal Rights and the Politics of Literary Representation.* Houndmills: Palgrave, 2002.
Singer, Peter. *Animal Liberation.* New York: Harper Collins, 1975.
———, ed. *In Defense of Animals: The Second Wave.* Oxford: Basil Blackwell, 2006.
Stamp Dawkins, Marian. *Through Our Eyes Only: The Search for Animal Consciousness.* Oxford: Oxford University Press, 1998.
Stein, Gertrude. *Paris, France.* New York: Charles Scribner's Sons, 1940.
Stewart, Joan Hinde. *Colette.* Updated ed. New York: Twayne, 1996.
Trachy, Carole Law. *The Mythology of Artemis and Her Role in Greek Popular Religion.* Ann Arbor: UMI, 1977.
Truc, Gonzague. *Madame Colette.* Paris: Corrêa, 1941.
Wharton, Edith. *Artemis to Actaeon and Other Verse.* New York: Charles Scribner's Sons, 1909.
———. "Kerfol." In *The Selected Stories of Edith Wharton,* ed. R.W.B. Lewis. New York: Charles Scribner's Sons, 1991.
Wolfe, Carey. *Animal Rites: American Culture, the Discourse of Species, and Posthumanist Theory.* Chicago: University of Chicago Press, 2003.
———, ed. *Zoontologies: The Question of the Animal.* Minneapolis: University of Minnesota Press, 2003.
Ziolkowski, Theodore. "Talking Dogs: The Caninization of Literature." In *Varieties of Literary Thematics,* 86–122. Princeton: Princeton University Press, 1983.

COVER DESIGN
Claudia Smelser

TEXT
10/13 Sabon

DISPLAY
Sabon

COMPOSITOR
Toppan Best-set Premedia Limited

PRINTER AND BINDER
IBT Global

www.ingramcontent.com/pod-product-compliance
Lightning Source LLC
Chambersburg PA
CBHW020655300426
44112CB00007B/395